Wonderful ways to prepare

ITALIAN
FOOD

by JO ANN SHIRLEY

with special thanks to
JANE DE TELIGA

OTHER TITLES IN THIS SERIES

1. HORS D'ŒUVRES & FIRST COURSES

2. SOUPS

3. MEAT

4. FISH & SEAFOOD

5. STEWS & CASSEROLES

6. SALADS

7. DESSERTS

8. CAKES & COOKIES

9. BARBECUES

10. ITALIAN FOOD

Wonderful ways to prepare

ITALIAN FOOD

PLAYMORE INC NEW YORK USA
UNDER ARRANGEMENT WITH
I. WALDMAN & SON INC

AYERS & JAMES PTY LTD
CROWS NEST AUSTRALIA

STAFFORD PEMBERTON PUBLISHING
KNUTSFORD UNITED KINGDOM

FIRST PUBLISHED 1978

PUBLISHED IN THE USA
BY PLAYMORE INC.
UNDER ARRANGEMENT WITH I. WALDMAN & SON INC.

PUBLISHED IN AUSTRALIA
BY AYERS & JAMES PTY. LTD.
CROWS NEST.   AUSTRALIA

PUBLISHED IN THE UNITED KINGDOM
BY STAFFORD PEMBERTON PUBLISHING
KNUTSFORD CHESIRE

ISBN 0 86908 063 6

OVEN TEMPERATURE GUIDE

Description	Gas		Electric		Mark
	C	F	C	F	
Cool	100	200	110	225	¼
Very Slow	120	250	120	250	½
Slow	150	300	150	300	1-2
Moderately slow	160	325	170	340	3
Moderate	180	350	200	400	4
Moderately hot	190	375	220	425	5-6
Hot	200	400	230	450	6-7
Very hot	230	450	250	475	8-9

LIQUID MEASURES

IMPERIAL	METRIC
1 teaspoon	5 ml
1 tablespoon	20 ml
2 fluid ounces (¼ cup)	62.5 ml
4 fluid ounces (½ cup)	125 ml
8 fluid ounces (1 cup)	250 ml
1 pint (16 ounces — 2 cups)*	500 ml

* (The imperial pint is equal to 20 fluid ounces.)

SOLID MEASURES

AVOIRDUPOIS	METRIC
1 ounce	30 g
4 ounces (¼ lb)	125 g
8 ounces (½ lb)	250 g
12 ounces (¾ lb)	375 g
16 ounces (1 lb)	500 g
24 ounces (1½ lb)	750 g
32 ounces (2 lb)	1000 g (1 kg)

CUP AND SPOON REPLACEMENTS FOR OUNCES

INGREDIENT	½ oz	1 oz	2 oz	3 oz	4 oz	5 oz	6 oz	7 oz	8 oz
Almonds, ground	2 T	¼ C	½ C	¾ C	1¼ C	1⅓ C	1⅔ C	2 C	2¼ C
slivered	6 t	¼ C	½ C	¾ C	1 C	1⅓ C	1⅔ C	2 C	2¼ C
whole	2 T	¼ C	⅓ C	½ C	¾ C	1 C	1¼ C	1⅓ C	1½ C
Apples, dried whole	3 T	½ C	1 C	1⅓ C	2 C	2⅓ C	2¾ C	3⅓ C	3¾ C
Apricots, chopped	2 T	¼ C	½ C	¾ C	1 C	1¼ C	1½ C	1¾ C	2 C
whole	2 T	3 T	½ C	⅔ C	1 C	1¼ C	1⅓ C	1½ C	1¾ C
Arrowroot	1 T	2 T	⅓ C	½ C	⅔ C	¾ C	1 C	1¼ C	1⅓ C
Baking Powder	1 T	2 T	⅓ C	½ C	⅔ C	¾ C	1 C	1 C	1¼ C
Baking Soda	1 T	2 T	⅓ C	½ C	⅔ C	¾ C	1 C	1 C	1¼ C
Barley	1 T	2 T	¼ C	½ C	⅔ C	¾ C	1 C	1 C	1¼ C
Breadcrumbs, dry	2 T	¼ C	½ C	¾ C	1 C	1¼ C	1½ C	1¾ C	2 C
soft	¼ C	½ C	1 C	1½ C	2 C	2½ C	3 C	3⅔ C	4¼ C
Biscuit Crumbs	2 T	¼ C	½ C	¾ C	1¼ C	1⅓ C	1⅔ C	2 C	2¼ C
Butter	3 t	6 t	¼ C	⅓ C	½ C	⅔ C	¾ C	1 C	1 C
Cheese, grated, lightly packed,									
natural cheddar	6 t	¼ C	½ C	¾ C	1 C	1¼ C	1½ C	1¾ C	2 C
Processed cheddar	5 t	2 T	⅓ C	⅔ C	¾ C	1 C	1¼ C	1½ C	1⅔ C
Parmesan, Romano	6 t	¼ C	½ C	¾ C	1 C	1⅓ C	1⅔ C	2 C	2¼ C
Cherries, candied, chopped	1 T	2 T	⅓ C	½ C	¾ C	1 C	1 C	1⅓ C	1½ C
whole	1 T	2 T	⅓ C	½ C	⅔ C	¾ C	1 C	1¼ C	1⅓ C
Cocoa	2 T	¼ C	½ C	¾ C	1¼ C	1⅓ C	1⅔ C	2 C	2¼ C
Coconut, desiccated	2 T	⅓ C	⅔ C	1 C	1⅓ C	1⅔ C	2 C	2⅓ C	2⅔ C
shredded	⅓ C	⅔ C	1¼ C	1¾ C	2½ C	3 C	3⅔ C	4⅓ C	5 C
Cornstarch	6 t	3 T	½ C	⅔ C	1 C	1¼ C	1½ C	1⅔ C	2 C
Corn Syrup	2 t	1 T	2 T	¼ C	⅓ C	½ C	½ C	⅔ C	⅔ C
Coffee, ground	2 T	⅓ C	⅔ C	1 C	1⅓ C	1⅔ C	2 C	2⅓ C	2⅔ C
instant	3 T	½ C	1 C	1⅓ C	1¾ C	2¼ C	2⅔ C	3 C	3½ C
Cornflakes	½ C	1 C	2 C	3 C	4¼ C	5¼ C	6¼ C	7⅓ C	8⅓ C
Cream of Tartar	1 T	2 T	⅓ C	½ C	⅔ C	¾ C	1 C	1 C	1¼ C
Currants	1 T	2 T	⅓ C	⅔ C	¾ C	1 C	1¼ C	1½ C	1⅔ C
Custard Powder	6 t	3 T	½ C	⅔ C	1 C	1¼ C	1½ C	1⅔ C	2 C
Dates, chopped	1 T	2 T	⅓ C	⅔ C	¾ C	1 C	1¼ C	1½ C	1⅔ C
whole, pitted	1 T	2 T	⅓ C	½ C	¾ C	1 C	1¼ C	1⅓ C	1½ C
Figs, chopped	1 T	2 T	⅓ C	½ C	¾ C	1 C	1 C	1⅓ C	1½ C
Flour, all-purpose or cake	6 t	¼ C	½ C	¾ C	1 C	1¼ C	1½ C	1¾ C	2 C
wholemeal	6 t	3 T	½ C	⅔ C	1 C	1¼ C	1⅓ C	1⅔ C	1¾ C
Fruit, mixed	1 T	2 T	⅓ C	½ C	¾ C	1 C	1¼ C	1⅓ C	1½ C
Gelatine	5 t	2 T	⅓ C	½ C	¾ C	1 C	1 C	1¼ C	1½ C
Ginger, crystallised pieces	1 T	2 T	⅓ C	½ C	¾ C	1 C	1¼ C	1⅓ C	1½ C
ground	6 t	⅓ C	½ C	¾ C	1¼ C	1½ C	1¾ C	2 C	2¼ C
preserved, heavy syrup	1 T	2 T	⅓ C	½ C	⅔ C	¾ C	1 C	1 C	1¼ C
Glucose, liquid	2 t	1 T	2 T	¼ C	⅓ C	½ C	½ C	⅔ C	⅔ C
Haricot Beans	1 T	2 T	⅓ C	½ C	⅔ C	¾ C	1 C	1 C	1¼ C

In this table, t represents teaspoonful, T represents tablespoonful and C represents cupful.

CUP AND SPOON REPLACEMENTS FOR OUNCES (Cont.)

INGREDIENT	½ oz	1 oz	2 oz	3 oz	4 oz	5 oz	6 oz	7 oz	8 oz
Honey	2 t	1 T	2 T	¼ C	⅓ C	½ C	½ C	⅔ C	⅔ C
Jam	2 t	1 T	2 T	¼ C	⅓ C	½ C	½ C	⅔ C	¾ C
Lentils	1 T	2 T	⅓ C	½ C	⅔ C	¾ C	1 C	1 C	1¼ C
Macaroni (see pasta)									
Milk Powder, full cream	2 T	¼ C	½ C	¾ C	1¼ C	1⅓ C	1⅔ C	2 C	2¼ C
non fat	2 T	⅓ C	¾ C	1¼ C	1½ C	2 C	2⅓ C	2¾ C	3¼ C
Nutmeg	6 t	3 T	½ C	⅔ C	¾ C	1 C	1¼ C	1½ C	1⅔ C
Nuts, chopped	6 t	¼ C	½ C	¾ C	1 C	1¼ C	1½ C	1¾ C	2 C
Oatmeal	1 T	2 T	½ C	⅔ C	¾ C	1 C	1¼ C	1½ C	1⅔ C
Olives, whole	1 T	2 T	⅓ C	⅔ C	¾ C	1 C	1¼ C	1½ C	1⅔ C
sliced	1 T	2 T	⅓ C	⅔ C	¾ C	1 C	1¼ C	1½ C	1⅔ C
Pasta, short (e.g. macaroni)	1 T	2 T	⅓ C	⅔ C	¾ C	1 C	1¼ C	1½ C	1⅔ C
Peaches, dried & whole	1 T	2 T	⅓ C	⅔ C	¾ C	1 C	1¼ C	1½ C	1⅔ C
chopped	6 t	¼ C	½ C	¾ C	1 C	1¼ C	1½ C	1¾ C	2 C
Peanuts, shelled, raw, whole	1 T	2 T	⅓ C	½ C	¾ C	1 C	1¼ C	1⅓ C	1½ C
roasted	1 T	2 T	⅓ C	⅔ C	¾ C	1 C	1¼ C	1½ C	1⅔ C
Peanut Butter	3 t	6 t	3 T	⅓ C	½ C	½ C	⅔ C	¾ C	1 C
Peas, split	1 T	2 T	⅓ C	½ C	⅔ C	¾ C	1 C	1 C	1¼ C
Peel, mixed	1 T	2 T	⅓ C	½ C	¾ C	1 C	1 C	1¼ C	1½ C
Potato, powder	1 T	2 T	¼ C	⅓ C	½ C	⅔ C	¾ C	1 C	1¼ C
flakes	¼ C	½ C	1 C	1⅓ C	2 C	2⅓ C	2¾ C	3⅓ C	3¾ C
Prunes, chopped	1 T	2 T	⅓ C	½ C	⅔ C	¾ C	1 C	1¼ C	1⅓ C
whole pitted	1 T	2 T	⅓ C	½ C	⅔ C	¾ C	1 C	1 C	1¼ C
Raisins	2 T	¼ C	⅓ C	½ C	¾ C	1 C	1 C	1⅓ C	1½ C
Rice, short grain, raw	1 T	2 T	¼ C	½ C	⅔ C	¾ C	1 C	1 C	1¼ C
long grain, raw	1 T	2 T	⅓ C	½ C	¾ C	1 C	1¼ C	1⅓ C	1½ C
Rice Bubbles	⅔ C	1¼ C	2½ C	3⅔ C	5 C	6¼ C	7½ C	8¾ C	10 C
Rolled Oats	2 T	⅓ C	⅔ C	1 C	1⅓ C	1¾ C	2 C	2½ C	2¾ C
Sago	2 T	¼ C	⅓ C	½ C	¾ C	1 C	1 C	1¼ C	1½ C
Salt, common	3 t	6 t	¼ C	⅓ C	½ C	⅔ C	¾ C	1 C	1 C
Semolina	1 T	2 T	⅓ C	½ C	¾ C	1 C	1 C	1⅓ C	1½ C
Spices	6 t	3 T	¼ C	⅓ C	½ C	½ C	⅔ C	¾ C	1 C
Sugar, plain	3 t	6 t	¼ C	⅓ C	½ C	⅔ C	¾ C	1 C	1 C
confectioners'	1 T	2 T	⅓ C	½ C	¾ C	1 C	1 C	1¼ C	1½ C
moist brown	1 T	2 T	⅓ C	½ C	¾ C	1 C	1 C	1⅓ C	1½ C
Tapioca	1 T	2 T	⅓ C	½ C	⅔ C	¾ C	1 C	1¼ C	1⅓ C
Treacle	2 t	1 T	2 T	¼ C	⅓ C	½ C	½ C	⅔ C	⅔ C
Walnuts, chopped	2 T	¼ C	½ C	¾ C	1 C	1¼ C	1½ C	1¾ C	2 C
halved	2 T	⅓ C	⅔ C	1 C	1¼ C	1½ C	1¾ C	2¼ C	2½ C
Yeast, dried	6 t	3 T	½ C	⅔ C	1 C	1¼ C	1⅓ C	1⅔ C	1¾ C
compressed	3 t	6 t	3 T	⅓ C	½ C	½ C	⅔ C	¾ C	1 C

In this table, t represents teaspoonful, T represents tablespoonful and C represents cupful.

Contents

Appetizers & Salads

Antipasto

- 1 lettuce, washed, drained and dried
- 4 tomatoes, quartered
- 1 10 oz can tuna fish
- 1 14 oz can artichoke hearts, drained
- 8 slices salami
- 8 slices ham
- 8 radishes
- 8 black olives
- 1 tablespoon chopped parsley
- 1 tablespoon capers
- Italian Dressing

1. Place lettuce leaves on a large platter. Arrange the tomatoes, tuna fish, artichoke hearts, salami, ham and radishes on the lettuce. Sprinkle the olives, parsley and capers over it all.
2. Pour the Italian Dressing over the antipasto and allow to marinate for ½ hour before serving.

Italian Dressing

- ½ cup (125 ml) olive oil
- 3 anchovy fillets, mashed
- 2 tablespoons lemon juice
  salt and pepper to taste

Combine all the ingredients and mix well.

Rice and Shrimp Salad (Insalata di Riso e Scampi)

1 cup (210 g) uncooked rice
salt and pepper
oregano
marjoram
¼ cup (62.5 ml) olive oil

2 tablespoons lemon juice
2 scallions, sliced
½ lb (250 g) shrimp, peeled and chopped
2 tablespoons chopped parsley

1. Cook the rice in boiling salted water until just tender. Drain.
2. Season the rice with salt, pepper, oregano and marjoram.
3. Pour on the olive oil and lemon juice while still warm and mix in the sliced scallions. Cool.
4. When cool, mix in the chopped shrimp and the parsley.

Serves 4-6.

Tuna Fish with Onion (Tonno Sott'Olio con Cipolle)

1 large can tuna fish (packed in oil) (13 oz)
pepper
1 tablespoon capers

1 onion, chopped
1 tablespoon chopped parsley
1 tablespoon lemon juice

1. Drain the tuna but reserve the oil. Break up the tuna and place on individual dishes.
2. Sprinkle tuna with pepper, capers, chopped onion and parsley. Pour a little of the reserved oil mixed with the lemon juice over all.

Serves 4.

Hot Spinach Salad
(Insalata di Spinaci)

1 lb (500 g) spinach
½ cup (125 ml) olive oil
juice of one lemon
grated rind of one lemon

2 cloves garlic, crushed
salt and pepper
croutons

1. Wash the spinach very well, remove the white stalks, drain and thoroughly dry.
2. Heat together the oil, lemon juice, grated rind and garlic in a saucepan.
3. Put the spinach in a large salad bowl. Pour the heated sauce over it and toss gently but thoroughly.
4. Season to taste with salt and pepper and garnish with croutons.

Serves 4.

Green Bean Salad
(Insalata di Fagiolini)

1 lb (500 g) fresh green
   beans
Garlic Dressing
salt and pepper
lettuce leaves
1 tablespoon chopped parsley

1. Cook the beans, uncut, in boiling salted water for five minutes. Drain.
2. Toss in Garlic Dressing while still warm. Season to taste.
3. Serve on lettuce leaves and garnish with chopped parsley.

Serves 4-6.

Garlic Dressing

½ cup (125 ml) olive oil
juice of one lemon
salt and pepper
1 garlic clove, crushed

Combine all ingredients in a screw-top jar and shake well.

Anchovy with Tomatoes (Acciughe con Pomodori)

4 medium tomatoes
¾ lb (375 g) canned anchovy
   fillets
1 tablespoon capers
juice of one lemon
pepper

1. Slice tomatoes and arrange on a platter.
2. Place anchovy fillets on top of the tomatoes.
3. Sprinkle capers over the anchovies.
4. Combine the oil from the anchovy tin with the lemon juice and pepper to taste. Pour over the tomatoes and anchovies.

Serves 4.

Mushrooms in Vinegar (Funghi al Aceto)

½ lb (250 g) button mushrooms
1 tablespoon whole mixed spices
1 clove garlic
1 teaspoon salt
1½ cups (75 ml) wine vinegar

1. Wipe the mushrooms with a damp cloth.
2. Heat vinegar until just warm. Mix in spices, garlic and salt.
3. Put mushrooms in a sterilized glass jar. Pour the vinegar mixture over and stir well.
4. Cover jar tightly and allow to stand for about two days.

Serves 4.

Cauliflower Salad
(Insalata di Cavolfiore)

1 cauliflower
salt and pepper
Italian Dressing
4 anchovy fillets

2 tablespoons chopped parsley
¼ lb (125 g) black olives,
  pitted and chopped
3 tablespoons capers

1. Cook the cauliflower in boiling salted water until just tender. Do not overcook. Drain and cut into flowerets. Season with salt and pepper.
2. Arrange cauliflower on a dish and pour over Italian Dressing.
3. Sprinkle with chopped anchovy fillets, parsley, olives and capers.

Italian Dressing

Combine ½ cup (125 ml) olive oil with 3 tablespoons of lemon juice. Season with salt and pepper. Finely chopped herbs may also be added.

Green Salad
(Insalata Verde)

1 head lettuce
1 bunch watercress
3 stalks celery with leaves

1 head endive
¼ lb (125 g) green olives
Dressing

1. Wash, drain and dry all the ingredients.
2. Break up and put into a salad bowl.
3. Toss with Dressing and scatter pitted olives over the top.

Dressing

½ cup (125 ml) olive oil
2 tablespoons wine vinegar
juice of half a lemon
salt and pepper

Combine all ingredients in a screw-top jar and shake well.

Bean and Tuna Fish Salad
(Insalata di Fagioli e Tonno)

½ lb (250 g) dried beans
4 cups (1 liter) water
3 tablespoons olive oil
1 tablespoon lemon juice
1 teaspoon salt
¼ teaspoon black pepper
3 scallions, chopped (white and green parts)

2 tablespoons chopped parsley
1 tablespoon finely chopped chives
1 medium can of tuna fish, packed in oil

1. Combine the beans and the water and bring to a boil. Remove from heat and allow to stand for one hour. Reheat in the same water. Cook for about 1½ hours or until tender. Drain.
2. Blend together the oil, lemon juice, salt, pepper, scallions, parsley and chives. Add to the hot beans and mix well. Cool.
3. When ready to serve, break tuna fish into chunks and arrange on top of the bean mixture.

Serves 4-6.

Artichoke Hearts
(Cuori di Carciofi)

2 14 oz cans artichoke hearts, drained
4 tablespoons olive oil
2 tablespoons lemon juice

½ teaspoon oregano
salt and pepper
1 tablespoon capers, chopped

1. Drain the artichoke hearts and place in a bowl.
2. Combine the oil, lemon juice, oregano and salt and pepper to taste.
3. Pour over the artichoke hearts. Allow to marinate for several hours, tossing the artichoke hearts in the marinade occasionally.
4. Serve on lettuce and sprinkle with chopped capers.

Serves 6.

Fried Mozzarella Sandwiches

½ lb (250 g) Mozzarella cheese
2 eggs, beaten
salt and pepper
1 cup (250 ml) milk
8 slices stale white bread
oil for frying

1. Beat together the eggs, salt and pepper to taste and the milk.
2. Make four sandwiches of the Mozzarella cheese and stale bread. (Remove crusts.)
3. Dip the sandwiches in the egg and milk mixture. Press the edges together.
4. Heat the oil to a high heat. Fry the sandwiches on both sides until golden brown. Drain and serve immediately.

Serves 4.

Fried Mushrooms (Funghi Fritti)

½ lb (250 g) mushroom caps
salt
juice of one lemon
flour
2 eggs, beaten

bread crumbs
oregano
½ cup (125 g) butter
  or margarine

1. Sprinkle the mushrooms with salt and lemon juice.
2. Toss them in the flour and then in the beaten eggs. Roll in bread crumbs and oregano.
3. Melt butter or margarine in a frypan and fry mushrooms for five to ten minutes.
4. When ready to serve, drain the mushrooms.

Serves 6.

Prosciutto and Melon (Prosciutto e Melone)

cantaloupe
prosciutto (smoked ham),
thinly sliced
lemon wedges

1. Cut melon into thin wedges, removing the skin and seeds.
2. Either wrap the prosciutto around the melon or serve on the side of the dish.
3. Serve with wedges of lemon.

Marinated Mushrooms (Funghi all'Olio e Aglio)

1 lb (500 g) button mushrooms	**2 cloves garlic, crushed**
½ cup (125 ml) olive oil	**4 tablespoons water**
½ cup (125 ml) vinegar	**1 bay leaf**
5 peppercorns	

1. Wipe the mushrooms with a damp cloth.
2. Combine the oil, vinegar, peppercorns, garlic, water, bay leaf and salt in a saucepan. Bring to a boil. Reduce heat, cover and simmer for fifteen minutes.
3. Add the mushrooms and simmer for another five minutes, stirring occasionally. Remove from heat and allow mushrooms to cool in the marinade.
4. When ready to serve, drain the mushrooms.

Serves 6.

Soups

Pumpkin Soup
(Zuppa di Zucca)

1 lb (500 g) pumpkin
½ lb (250 g) potatoes
1 onion, chopped
⅓ cup (83 g) butter or
   margarine
2½ cups (625 ml) milk
salt and pepper

2 leeks, sliced
2½ cups (625 ml) chicken stock
½ cup (125 ml) cream
2 tablespoons chopped parsley

1. Peel and dice pumpkin and potatoes.
2. Melt half the butter or margarine in a saucepan and sauté the onion until golden brown.
3. Add the diced pumpkin and potatoes and milk. Bring to a boil, reduce heat and simmer for about 40 minutes.
4. Sieve or purée in an electric blender.
5. Season to taste with salt and pepper.
6. Sauté the leeks in the remaining butter or margarine.
7. Add to the soup with the chicken stock. Bring to a boil. Reduce heat and simmer for five minutes.
8. Before serving, stir in cream and chopped parsley.

Serves 6.

Minestrone

1 cup (200 g) dried kidney beans
3 tablespoons olive oil
1 clove garlic, chopped
1 large onion, chopped
1 cup canned tomatoes
1 cup shelled peas
2 tablespoons chopped parsley

1 celery stalk, chopped
1 carrot, chopped
1 large potato (raw), chopped
8 cups (2 liters) beef stock
salt and pepper
1 cup (200 g) uncooked rice

1. Cover the dried beans with water and soak overnight. Drain.
2. Put oil in a large saucepan, add garlic, onion and remaining vegetables. Cover and simmer for 15 minutes, stirring occasionally.
3. Add soaked beans, beef stock and salt and pepper to taste. Cover and simmer for 1-1½ hours or until beans are tender.
4. Add rice and simmer for another 15 minutes.

Serves 6.

Chopped Meat Minestrone (Minestrone di Carne)

1 lb (500 g) ground beef
2 medium onions, chopped
½ lb (250 g) tomatoes, peeled and chopped
1 cup fresh peas

½ cup string beans, cut in 1-inch (2½-cm) pieces
1 small carrot, chopped
salt and pepper

1. Brown the beef with the onions in a large saucepan, stirring constantly to break up meat.
2. Add tomatoes and simmer for about five minutes.
3. Add peas, beans and carrot and simmer for another five minutes.
4. Pour on enough cold water to cover. Season to taste with salt and pepper.
5. Cover and simmer until vegetables are tender.

Serves 6.

Peasant Minestrone
(Minestrone Rustica)

½ small cabbage, shredded
2 carrots, chopped
2 small onions, chopped
2 turnips, chopped
4 tablespoons chopped parsley
¼ lb (125 g) shelled peas
½ lb (250 g) string beans,
   cut up

½ lb (250 g) beef ribs
salt and pepper
8 cups (2 liters) boiling water
1 lb (500 g) Italian sausage,
   cut up
1 cup (120 g) grated Parmesan
   cheese

1. Put all the vegetables in a large saucepan with the beef ribs, salt and pepper and boiling water. Cover and cook over a low heat for about 1½ hours.
2. Remove meat from bone and return to soup.
3. Add sausage and cook for another ½ hour .
4. Serve with grated Parmesan cheese on top.

Serves 4-6.

Rice and Pea Soup
(Minestrone di Riso e Piselli)

⅓ cup (83 g) butter
2 slices bacon, chopped
1 slice ham, chopped
1 onion, minced
1½ tablespoons chopped
   parsley

2 lb (1 kg) fresh green peas
4 cups (1 liter) water
½ cup (105 g) uncooked rice
salt and pepper
4 tablespoons grated Parmesan
   cheese

1. Sauté the bacon, ham and onion in the butter until golden brown.
2. Add peas and parsley and cook for five minutes, stirring constantly.
3. Add the water and bring to a boil.
4. Stir in rice, salt and pepper to taste and cheese. Cook over a medium heat until rice is tender.

Serves 6.

Chicken Soup with Eggs (Zuppa alla Pavese)

3½ tablespoons (70 g) butter
    or margarine
6 slices bread without crusts
7 cups (1¾ liters) chicken
    stock

6 eggs
3 tablespoons grated Parmesan
    cheese

1. Melt the butter or margarine in a large frypan and sauté the bread until it is golden brown on both sides. Set aside.
2. Pour chicken stock into a large but shallow saucepan. Bring to a boil. Reduce heat to simmering point.
3. Carefully break eggs, one at a time, into the simmering (not boiling) stock. Cook eggs for about four minutes.
4. Remove eggs from the stock and put into individual soup bowls. Spoon stock over the eggs.
5. Sprinkle the cheese on the fried bread, cut into small squares and put on top of soup.

Serves 6.

Chicken Soup with Eggs and Cheese (Stracciatella)

4 eggs
4 tablespoons grated Parmesan
    cheese
1 tablespoon chopped parsley

pinch of nutmeg
1 teaspoon salt
8 cups (2 liters) chicken stock

1. Lightly beat the eggs. Add the cheese, parsley, nutmeg and salt.
2. Bring the chicken stock to a boil in a large saucepan.
3. Pour in the egg mixture and stir constantly with a fork or a whisk. Cook for about three minutes.

Serves 6.

Chicken Soup
(Zuppa di Pollo)

4 lb (2 kg) stewing chicken
   pieces
2 celery stalks with leaves,
   chopped

3 tablespoons chopped parsley
2 carrots, whole
1 large tomato
salt and pepper

1. Put the chicken pieces in a large saucepan and cover with cold water. Bring to a boil.
2. Add vegetables and salt and pepper to taste. Cover and simmer for about 2-2½ hours.
3. Strain broth. If desired you may remove meat from the bones and return to the soup.

Serves 6.

Chick Peas with Rice
(Riso con Ceci)

1 lb (500 g) dried chick peas
2 tablespoons chopped parsley
salt and pepper
1 cup (210 g) uncooked rice
2 tablespoons olive oil

1. Cover chick peas with water and soak overnight.
2. Drain. Put in a saucepan with enough water to cover and cook over a high heat for one hour, adding more water to keep peas covered. Reduce heat and cook for another hour. Add more water when necessary.
3. Add parsley, salt and pepper to taste and rice. Cook until peas and rice are tender.
4. Remove from heat and stir in the olive oil.

Serves 6.

Beef Soup
(Zuppa)

1½ lb (750 g) chuck steak
1 lb (500 g) soup bones with marrow
1 can tomatoes
2 carrots
2 medium onions, quartered

3 sprigs parsley
1 celery stalk with leaves, halved
salt and pepper
½ lb (250 g) pastina

1. Place beef and bones in a large saucepan and cover with cold water. Bring to a boil and skim top with a spoon.
2. Add whole vegetables to the meat. Season to taste with salt and pepper.
3. Cover and cook over a low heat for 2-2½ hours or until meat is tender.
4. Remove meat, bones and vegetables from the soup. Cut meat into small pieces. Purée the vegetables and return both the meat and the vegetables to the soup.
5. Add pastina and cook for another 15 minutes.

Serves 6.

Zucchini Soup
(Zuppa di Zucchini)

1½ lb (750 g) zucchini, sliced
¼ cup (62.5 g) butter or margarine
2 onions, sliced
salt
8 cups (2 liters) water

4 eggs
¼ cup (30 g) grated Parmesan cheese
pepper
1 teaspoon basil

1. Melt the butter or margarine in a saucepan and sauté the onions until golden brown.
2. Add the zucchini and brown.
3. Season with salt and add the water. Bring to a boil. Reduce heat and simmer, covered, for ½ hour.
4. Beat the eggs with the cheese, pepper and basil. Bring the soup back to a boil and, stirring constantly, add the egg and cheese mixture. Simmer for a few minutes until the eggs are cooked. Serve topped with Parmesan cheese.

Serves 6.

Fish Soup
(Zuppa di Pesce)

5 cups (1.2 liters) fish
  stock
2 stalks celery, chopped
1 onion, sliced
2 tablespoons vinegar
1 tablespoon salt
½ lb (250 g) shrimp, shelled
2 lb (1 kg) mixed fish, cut
  into bite-size pieces
⅓ cup olive oil (83 ml)

2 cloves garlic, crushed
2 bay leaves
½ teaspoon thyme
1 teaspoon basil
2 tablespoons chopped parsley
1 cup (250 ml) dry white wine
½ lb (250 g) tomatoes, peeled
  and chopped
salt and pepper

1. Make fish stock by boiling fish heads and shrimp shells in water for about ten minutes. Strain.
2. Add celery, onion, vinegar and salt to fish stock. Simmer, covered, for about ten minutes. Strain broth and set aside.
3. Sauté the shrimp and the fish in the oil with the garlic, bay leaves, thyme, basil and parsley for about five minutes, stirring constantly.
4. Add fish stock, wine, tomatoes and salt and pepper to taste. Bring to a boil. Reduce heat, cover and simmer for about 20 minutes.

Serves 6-8.

Quick Beef Soup

1½ lb (750 g) round steak
1 carrot
1 tomato

1 celery stalk with leaves
salt and pepper
¼ lb (125 g) fine noodles

1. Put meat in a large saucepan. Cover with cold water and bring to a boil. Skim surface.
2. Add vegetables and salt and pepper to taste.
3. Cover and simmer for about 45 minutes or until meat is tender.
4. Remove meat and vegetables from soup and add noodles. Cook for about 10 minutes.
5. Cut meat into small pieces and return to the soup. Reheat.

Serves 6.

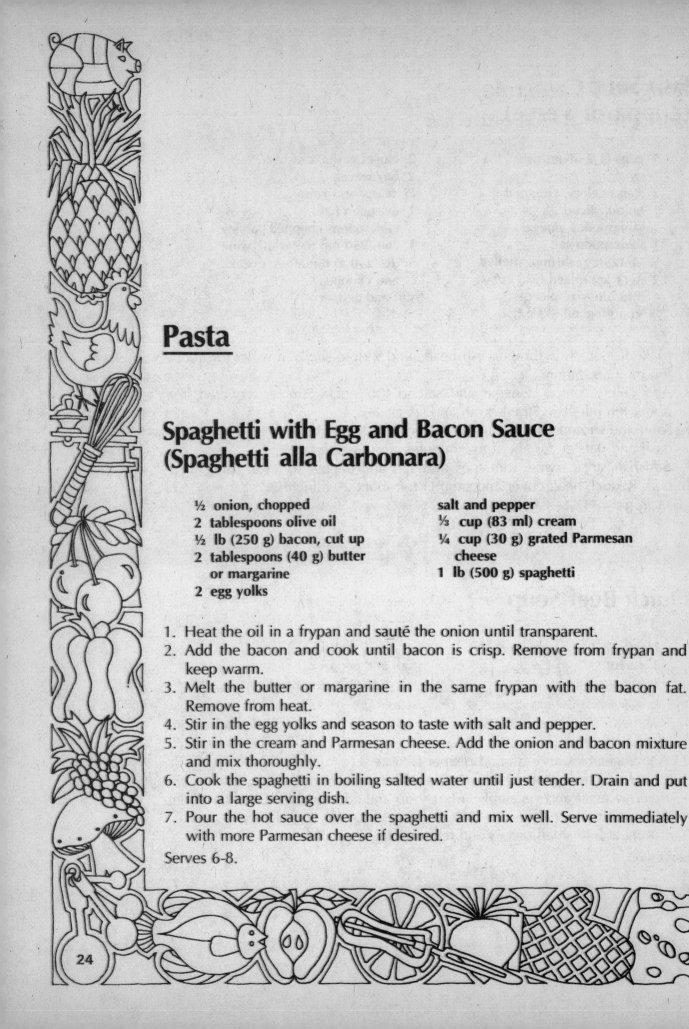

Pasta

Spaghetti with Egg and Bacon Sauce
(Spaghetti alla Carbonara)

½ onion, chopped
2 tablespoons olive oil
½ lb (250 g) bacon, cut up
2 tablespoons (40 g) butter
  or margarine
2 egg yolks

salt and pepper
⅓ cup (83 ml) cream
¼ cup (30 g) grated Parmesan
  cheese
1 lb (500 g) spaghetti

1. Heat the oil in a frypan and sauté the onion until transparent.
2. Add the bacon and cook until bacon is crisp. Remove from frypan and keep warm.
3. Melt the butter or margarine in the same frypan with the bacon fat. Remove from heat.
4. Stir in the egg yolks and season to taste with salt and pepper.
5. Stir in the cream and Parmesan cheese. Add the onion and bacon mixture and mix thoroughly.
6. Cook the spaghetti in boiling salted water until just tender. Drain and put into a large serving dish.
7. Pour the hot sauce over the spaghetti and mix well. Serve immediately with more Parmesan cheese if desired.

Serves 6-8.

Spaghetti Casserole
(Spaghetti in Casseruola)

2 tablespoons olive oil	salt and pepper
1 lb (500 g) Italian sausage, cut into 1 inch (2½-cm) pieces	¾ lb (375 g) cooked spaghetti
1 onion, chopped	½ lb (250 g) Mozzarella cheese, sliced
¼ lb (125 g) mushrooms, sliced	3 tablespoons grated Parmesan cheese
¼ lb (125 g) tomatoes, peeled and seeded	

1. Brown the sausage in the oil over a medium heat for about ten minutes.
2. Add onion, mushrooms and tomatoes. Season to taste with salt and pepper and cook, uncovered, over a low heat for about one hour, stirring occasionally.
3. Put cooked spaghetti in a baking dish and cover with the slices of Mozzarella cheese.
4. Pour sauce over the cheese and sprinkle with grated cheese.
5. Bake in a 350°F (180°C) oven for about ten minutes.

Serves 6-8.

Spaghetti Marinara

3 tablespoons olive oil	1 tablespoon chopped fresh basil
1 clove garlic, crushed	salt and pepper
2 lb (1 kg) tomatoes, peeled and seeded	¾ lb (375 g) cooked spaghetti
2 tablespoons chopped parsley	¼ cup (30 g) grated Parmesan cheese

1. Sauté the garlic in the oil for about two minutes.
2. Add tomatoes and break up with a fork. Blend well with the garlic.
3. Sprinkle with parsley and basil. Add salt and pepper to taste and cook, uncovered, over a low heat for about one hour, stirring occasionally.
4. Put cooked spaghetti in a baking dish and mix well. Sprinkle with grated cheese and serve immediately.

Serves 6-8.

25

Spaghetti with Oil and Garlic
(Spaghetti all'Olio e Aglio)

½ lb (250 g) spaghetti
½ cup (125 ml) olive oil
3 cloves garlic, crushed
2 tablespoons chopped parsley

1. Cook the spaghetti in boiling salted water until just tender.
2. Sauté the garlic in the olive oil until golden brown.
3. Drain the spaghetti and put in a serving bowl.
4. Pour the oil and garlic over the spaghetti and mix thoroughly.
5. Sprinkle with parsley and serve immediately.

Serves 4.

Spaghetti with Peas
(Spaghetti con Piselli)

¼ lb (125 g) bacon, chopped
1 onion, chopped
1 clove garlic, crushed
½ stalk celery, chopped
2 tablespoons chopped parsley
¼ cup (62.5 ml) olive oil
1½ lb (750 g) peas, shelled
½ cup (125 ml) beef stock

1 tomato, peeled and chopped
2 tablespoons chopped fresh basil
   or 1 teaspoon ground basil
salt and pepper
1 lb (500 g) spaghetti
1 tablespoon (20 g) butter
   or margarine
grated Parmesan cheese

1. Mix together the bacon, onion, garlic, celery and parsley and sauté in the olive oil for about five minutes.
2. Add peas and beef stock and cook, covered, until peas are tender. Stir occasionally.
3. Add tomatoes, basil and salt and pepper to taste. Cook for five minutes.
4. Cook spaghetti in boiling salted water until just tender. Drain. Stir in one tablespoon of butter or margarine.
5. Pour the vegetable sauce over the spaghetti and toss thoroughly. Sprinkle with Parmesan cheese.

Serves 8.

Spaghettini with Butter (Spaghettini al Burro)

¾ lb (375 g) uncooked spaghettini
12 cups (3 liters) water
salt and pepper
½ cup (125 g) butter
½ cup (60 g) grated Parmesan
   cheese

1. Cook spaghettini in boiling salted water until tender. Drain and place in a serving dish.
2. Melt butter and pour over the spaghettini.
3. Season with salt and pepper to taste. Add cheese and mix thoroughly. Serve immediately.

Serves 6.

Vermicelli with Zucchini (Vermicelli con Zucchini)

1½ lb (750 g) zucchini
¼ cup (62.5 ml) olive oil
1 onion, chopped
1 lb (500 g) tomatoes, peeled
   and chopped
2 cups (500 ml) water

2 tablespoons chopped fresh
   basil
½ lb (250 g) vermicelli,
   broken into pieces
salt and pepper

1. Slice the zucchini into ½-inch (one-cm) pieces.
2. Sauté the onion in the oil until golden brown.
3. Add tomatoes and simmer for five minutes.
4. Add water and bring to a boil.
5. Add zucchini and basil and cook for five minutes.
6. Stir in vermicelli and cook over a low heat until tender, stirring occasionally. Season with salt and pepper to taste.

Serves 4.

Rice Milanese
(Risotto Milanese)

¼ cup (62.5 g) butter
  or margarine
1 onion, finely chopped
1 cup (210 g) uncooked rice
3 cups (750 ml) chicken stock

¼ teaspoon saffron
2 tablespoons boiling water
¼ cup (30 g) grated Parmesan
  cheese
salt and pepper

1. Sauté the onion in the butter or margarine over a low heat until golden brown.
2. Add rice and cook for about ten minutes, stirring constantly.
3. Add one cup of stock and mix well.
4. Dissolve the saffron in the two tablespoons of boiling water.
5. Add the remainder of the stock and the saffron. Season to taste with salt and pepper and mix thoroughly. Cook over a low heat for 15 minutes.
6. Add half the cheese and cook for another 20 minutes. Stir in more stock if necessary.
7. Just before serving, add the rest of the cheese.

Serves 4.

Rice with Mushrooms
(Risotto di Funghi)

2 onions, chopped finely
2 tablespoons (40 g) butter
  or margarine
1 lb (500 g) mushrooms,
  quartered
1 cup (250 ml) dry white wine

1 lb (500 g) rice, uncooked
5 cups (1.2 liters) chicken
  stock
½ cup (60 g) grated Parmesan
  cheese
cream

1. Sauté the onions in the butter or margarine until transparent.
2. Add the mushrooms and toss until the mushrooms are coated with the butter.
3. Add the wine and cook until the wine had evaporated.
4. Stir in the rice and add the stock. Cover and cook over a low heat for about twenty minutes or until rice is cooked and stock has been absorbed.
5. Stir in half the cheese and a little cream to moisten.
6. Serve with the remaining cheese sprinkled on top.

Rice with Peas
(Risi e Bisi)

1 tablespoon (20 g) butter
or margarine
3 tablespoons olive oil
8 spring onions
¾ lb (375 g) rice
¼ lb (125 g) ham, chopped

5 cups (1.2 liters) chicken stock
1 lb (500 g) shelled peas
½ cup (125 ml) cream
½ cup (60 g) grated Parmesan cheese
butter or margarine

1. Sauté the chopped onions in the butter or margarine and olive oil until transparent.
2. Add the rice and mix thoroughly. Stir in the ham.
3. Mix in the stock and bring to a boil. Add the peas, cover and cook over a low heat for about twenty minutes or until rice is cooked and the stock is absorbed.
4. Before serving, mix in the cream, half the cheese and a little butter or margarine.
5. Sprinkle with the remaining cheese.

Serves 4-6.

Rice in White Wine
(Risotto in Vino Bianco)

3 tablespoons (60 g) butter
or margarine
1 onion, minced
1 lb (500 g) rice
1 cup (250 ml) dry white wine

4 cups (1 liter) chicken stock
2 tablespoons (40 g) butter
or margarine
½ cup (60 g) grated Parmesan
cheese

1. Sauté the onion in the three tablespoons of butter or margarine until golden.
2. Stir in the rice and cook until the rice becomes transparent.
3. Add the wine and cook until the wine is evaporated.
3. Add ½ cup of boiling stock at a time, stirring constantly and cooking until the stock has been absorbed before adding next ½ cup.
5. When rice is cooked (about 20 minutes), add the two tablespoons of butter or margarine and the Parmesan cheese. Mix thoroughly.

Serves 6.

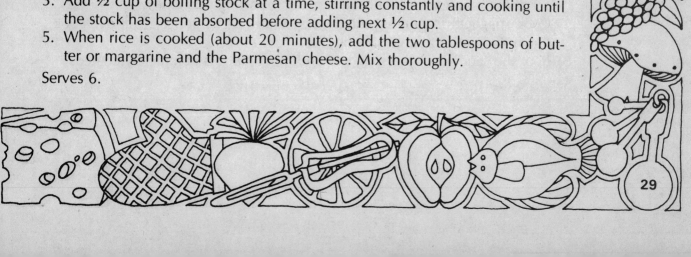

Macaroni with Ricotta Sauce
(Salsa di Ricotta con Pasta)

1 medium onion, chopped	1½ cups (375 ml) water
4 tablespoons olive oil	salt and pepper
1 lb (500 g) ricotta cheese	½ lb (250 g) short macaroni
1 cup (250 ml) tomato purée	4 tablespoons grated Romano
½ cup (125 g) tomato paste	cheese

1. Sauté the onion in the olive oil until golden brown.
2. Add ricotta, tomato purée, tomato paste and water and mix thoroughly.
3. Season with salt and pepper to taste and cook over a low heat for about one hour, stirring occasionally.
4. Cook macaroni in boiling salted water until tender. Drain. Put into a serving dish.
5. Pour sauce over the macaroni and sprinkle with grated cheese.

Serves 4-6.

Spaghetti with Anchovies Milanese
(Pasta alla Milanese con Acciughe)

1 onion, minced	4 cups (1 liter) water
2 tablespoons olive oil	2 tablespoons pine nuts
⅛ lb (60 g) canned anchovy	1 lb (500 g) spaghetti
fillets	salt and pepper
¾ cup (186 g) tomato paste	

1. Sauté the onion in olive oil until golden brown.
2. Add anchovies and oil from can to the onion and mash to a paste.
3. Add tomato paste and water and mix thoroughly.
4. Season with a little salt and pepper. Add pine nuts. Cook over a low heat for about one hour or until sauce is thick, stirring frequently.
5. Cook spaghetti in boiling salted water until just tender. Do not overcook. Drain and put in a large serving dish.
6. Pour the sauce over the spaghetti and mix until it is completely coated.

Serves 6-8.

Basic Pizza Dough

2¼ cups flour
½ teaspoon salt
1 tablespoon dried yeast
¾ cup (186 ml) warm water
olive oil

1. Sift flour into a warm bowl with the salt.
2. Put yeast into a small bowl and add the warm water. Allow to stand for five minutes, then mix until smooth.
3. Pour the yeast mixture into the flour with one tablespoon of olive oil. Mix with your hand to a stiff dough. Knead on a floured board for ten minutes.
4. Rub oil on the dough ball, place in an oiled bowl and put in a warm place until it has doubled in size.
5. Roll out to a thickness of ¼ inch (5 mm). Brush with a little olive oil before spreading with topping.

Roman-Style Pizza
(Pizza alla Romana)

Basic Pizza Dough
½ lb (250 g) Mozzarella
  cheese, sliced
½ cup (60 g) grated Parmesan
  cheese

¼ cup (62.5 ml) olive oil
2 onions, sliced
3 teaspoons chopped fresh
  basil

1. Arrange Mozzarella cheese on the rolled out pizza dough.
2. Sprinkle with Parmesan cheese and olive oil.
3. Lay sliced onions on top and sprinkle with fresh basil.
4. Bake in a 450°F (230°C) oven for about 25 minutes.
Serves 4-6.

31

Anchovy Pizza
(Pizza con Acciughe)

8 anchovy fillets,
   cut in small pieces
2 tablespoons olive oil
2 onions, thinly sliced
1½ lb (750 g) tomatoes,
   peeled and chopped

¼ cup (30 g) grated Parmesan
   cheese
salt and pepper
Basic Pizza Dough
   (see index)

1. Spread dough on an oiled baking sheet.
2. Brush the dough with a mixture of the olive oil and oil from the anchovy tin.
3. Arrange the anchovy fillets on the pizza dough.
4. Spread onions and tomatoes over the dough.
5. Sprinkle with cheese, salt and pepper.
6. Bake in a 450°F (230°C) oven for about 25 minutes.

Serves 4-6.

Super Pizza

1 tablespoon olive oil
1 medium onion, sliced
4 oz (125 g) tomato paste
1 cup (250 ml) water
½ lb (250 g) Italian sausage,
   chopped
2 slices bacon, diced
½ green pepper, chopped

¼ lb (125 g) mushrooms,
   sliced
½ lb (250 g) Mozzarella cheese,
   shredded
salt and pepper
oregano
Basic Pizza Dough
   (see index)

1. Sauté the onion in the olive oil until transparent.
2. Add the tomato paste and water and mix well. Cook uncovered for about 15 minutes.
3. Roll out and spread dough on an oiled baking sheet.
4. Cover dough with sausage, bacon, pepper, mushrooms, cheese and season with salt and pepper.
5. Add cooked tomato sauce and sprinkle with oregano.
6. Bake in a 450°F (230°C) oven for about 25 minutes.

Serves 4-6.

Pizza Napoletana

2 lb (1 kg) canned Italian
   tomatoes, chopped
salt and pepper
½ lb (250 g) Mozzarella
   cheese, sliced

8 anchovy fillets, chopped
½ teaspoon oregano
½ teaspoon basil
black olives, pitted and sliced
Pizza Dough (see index)

1. Place rolled out pizza dough on an oiled baking sheet.
2. Spread the tomatoes over the dough and sprinkle with salt and pepper.
3. Arrange the slices of Mozzarella cheese over the tomatoes. Put anchovies on top and sprinkle with oregano and basil. Garnish with black olive slices.
4. Bake in a 450°F (230°C) oven for about 30 minutes.

Serves 4-6.

Cheese Pizza
(Pizza al Formaggio)

1 cup (115 g) grated Parmesan
   cheese
1 cup (125 g) sharp cheese,
   grated

2 eggs, well beaten
salt and pepper
Pizza Dough (see index)

1. Roll out pizza dough and place on an oiled baking sheet.
2. Mix together with Parmesan cheese, cheese and eggs. Season with salt and pepper.
3. Spread cheese mixture over the pizza dough.
4. Bake in a 450°F (230°C) oven for about 25 minutes or until golden brown.

Serves 4-6.

Lasagne

2 tablespoons oil
2 onions, minced
1 lb (500 g) ground beef
1 clove garlic, crushed
1½ teaspoons salt
¼ teaspoon black pepper
½ teaspoon oregano
3 tablespoons chopped parsley

3 cups canned tomatoes
½ cup (125 ml) tomato purée
½ cup (125 g) tomato paste
½ cup (60 g) Parmesan cheese
½ lb (250 g) lasagna noodles
1 lb (500 g) Mozzarella cheese
1 lb (500 g) ricotta
or cottage cheese

1. Heat the oil and sauté the onions until golden brown.
2. Add the beef and cook for ten to fifteen minutes, stirring to break up the meat.
3. Mix in the garlic, salt, pepper, oregano, parsley, tomatoes, tomato purée, tomato paste and two tablespoons grated Parmesan cheese. Simmer, covered, for about 45 minutes.
4. Cook noodles in boiling salted water until tender. Drain and cover with cold water.
5. Arrange one-third of the meat sauce in a 8 x 12 inch (20 x 30 cm) baking dish. Cover with a layer of the lasagna noodles, then a layer of Mozzarella cheese, then a layer of ricotta or cottage cheese. Sprinkle with two tablespoons Parmesan cheese. Repeat layers ending with a layer of sauce and Parmesan.
6. Bake in a 350°F (180°C) oven about ½ hour.

Serves 6.

Ravioli

    4 cups sifted flour
    ½ teaspoon salt
    5 eggs
    ¼ cup (62.5 ml) warm water

1. Sift flour onto a large pastry board.
2. Make a well in the center and add salt, eggs and water. Mix thoroughly.
3. Knead the dough for about two minutes. Allow dough to stand for ten minutes.
4. Divide the dough into quantities that are easy to roll out. Roll each section out on a floured board to a thickness of ⅛ inch (3 mm). Cut into 2-inch (5-cm) rounds or squares and place a teaspoon of filling in the center. Cover with another circle or square and press edges together with a fork.
5. Cook in boiling salted water until dough is tender. Serve with sauce of your choice.

Chicken Filling

    2 cups cooked chicken, chopped
    1 egg
    ½ cup (60 g) grated Parmesan
       cheese
    1 tablespoon minced parsley
    1 cup cooked spinach, chopped
    salt and pepper

Combine all ingredients and mix thoroughly.

Ricotta Filling

    1 lb (500 g) ricotta
    2 eggs, beaten
    2 tablespoons minced parsley
    ¼ cup (30 g) grated Parmesan
       cheese
    salt and pepper

Thoroughly beat together all ingredients.

Parmesan Dumplings (Gnocchi di Parmigiano)

3 cups (750 ml) milk	2 cups (230 g) grated Parmesan
4 tablespoons (80 g) butter	cheese
or margarine	2 eggs
½ teaspoon salt	½ cup (125 g) butter
½ cup (85 g) semolina	or margarine, melted

1. Mix together the milk, butter or margarine and salt in a saucepan. Bring to a boil.
2. Slowly add the semolina to the milk, stirring constantly. Cook over a medium heat until thick.
3. Remove from heat and add one cup of cheese. Add eggs and mix well.
4. Pour the mixture onto a large plate and cool. (As it cools the mixture will harden.)
5. When it is hard, cut into small squares.
6. Grease the bottom of a baking sheet with some of the melted butter or margarine. Put a layer of the squares on the sheet, pour some melted butter or margarine over them and sprinkle with grated cheese. Repeat layers until all ingredients are used up. Season each layer with salt and pepper.
7. Bake in a 375°F (190°C) oven for about ½ hour.

Chicken Dumplings (Gnocchi con Pollo)

5 medium potatoes,	½ teaspoon nutmeg
peeled and cooked	1 cup flour
1 cup cooked chicken,	2 egg yolks
ground finely	salt and pepper
¼ cup (30 g) grated Parmesan	
cheese	

1. Mash the potatoes. Mix with the chicken, cheese, nutmeg, flour, egg yolks and salt and pepper to taste.
2. Place on a board and knead until smooth. Add more flour if necessary.
3. Roll out dough to a thickness of ½ inch (one cm). Cut into one-inch (2½-cm) squares.
4. Cook in boiling salted water for about ten minutes. Drain and serve with sauce of your choice.

Spinach and Cheese Dumplings (Gnocchi di Spinaci e Ricotta)

1 lb (500 g) spinach
salt and pepper
¼ cup (62.5 g) butter
   or margarine
½ lb (250 g) Ricotta cheese

2 cups flour
2 eggs
¼ cup (62.5 g) melted butter
Parmesan cheese

1. Wash the spinach thoroughly and cut out the white core. Cook, covered, in a saucepan with salt and pepper to taste. (Do not add any extra water.) Drain and chop finely. Rub through a fine sieve.
2. Cream the ¼ cup butter or margarine with the Ricotta cheese and add to the spinach. Mix very well.
3. Beat in the flour, eggs and salt and pepper to taste.
4. With floured hands, shape into small balls.
5. Drop a couple at a time into boiling salted water. The dumplings are cooked when they rise to the top. Remove and keep warm while you cook the rest of the dumplings.
6. Pour the melted butter over the dumplings and sprinkle with Parmesan cheese.

Serves 6.

Polenta

1 lb (500 g) polenta
   (corn meal)
9 cups (2.2 liters) water
salt

1. In a large saucepan bring water to a boil and add salt.
2. Slowly add the polenta, stirring constantly.
3. Cook over a medium heat, keeping mixture at a low boil, stirring frequently for about one hour.
4. When very thick, turn out onto a floured board. Traditionally, polenta is cut with a string or with a wooden polenta knife. Polenta may be eaten plain with butter and cheese or with a meat or tomato sauce.

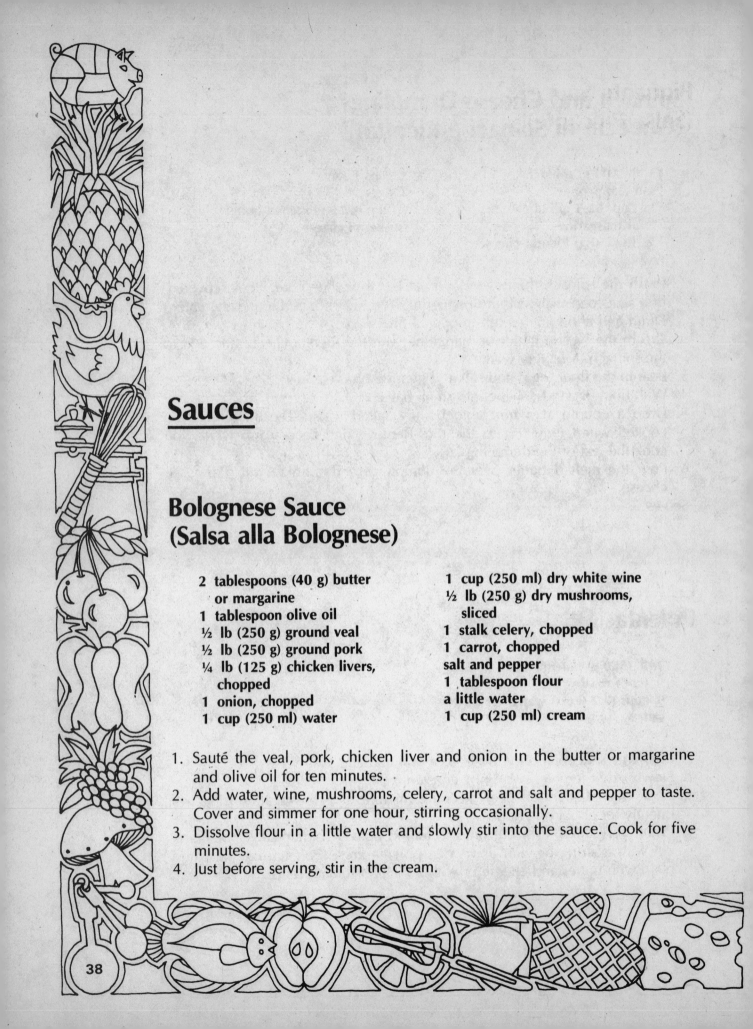

Sauces

Bolognese Sauce (Salsa alla Bolognese)

2 tablespoons (40 g) butter or margarine
1 tablespoon olive oil
½ lb (250 g) ground veal
½ lb (250 g) ground pork
¼ lb (125 g) chicken livers, chopped
1 onion, chopped
1 cup (250 ml) water

1 cup (250 ml) dry white wine
½ lb (250 g) dry mushrooms, sliced
1 stalk celery, chopped
1 carrot, chopped
salt and pepper
1 tablespoon flour
a little water
1 cup (250 ml) cream

1. Sauté the veal, pork, chicken liver and onion in the butter or margarine and olive oil for ten minutes.
2. Add water, wine, mushrooms, celery, carrot and salt and pepper to taste. Cover and simmer for one hour, stirring occasionally.
3. Dissolve flour in a little water and slowly stir into the sauce. Cook for five minutes.
4. Just before serving, stir in the cream.

Piquante Sauce
(Salsa Piccante)

3 tablespoons olive oil
2 tablespoons wine vinegar
½ cup (125 g) tomato paste
salt and pepper

1 teaspoon sugar
1 teaspoon prepared mustard
3 hard-boiled egg yolks, mashed

1. Combine oil and vinegar in a saucepan.
2. Add the tomato paste, salt and pepper and sugar and mix well.
3. Bring to a boil. Reduce heat and simmer, uncovered, for ten minutes. Remove from heat.
4. Stir in the mustard and egg yolks. Serve chilled.

Garlic Sauce
(Salsa di Aglio)

4 cloves garlic, crushed
½ teaspoon salt
1 egg yolk
⅓ cup (83 ml) olive oil
juice of two lemons
1 teaspoon oregano

1. Mash garlic to a paste with the salt.
2. Beat the egg yolk and add to the garlic. Mix well.
3. Add the olive oil a little at a time to the garlic and egg yolk mixture.
4. Mix in the lemon juice and oregano.
(If desired, whisk in an electric blender.)

39

Pine Nut Sauce
(Salsa di Pignoli)

4 tablespoons pine nuts
½ cup (125 ml) wine vinegar
1 cup (250 ml) water
2 tablespoons chopped parsley
salt and pepper

Combine all ingredients and cook for about ten minutes over a medium heat.

Tomato Sauce
(Salsa di Pomodoro)

4 lb (2 kg) ripe tomatoes
¼ cup (62.5 ml) olive oil
2 cloves garlic, crushed
1 stalk celery, chopped
1 carrot, finely chopped

1 teaspoon sugar
1 tablespoon chopped fresh
basil
1 tablespoon chopped parsley
salt and pepper

1. Chop tomatoes and cook in a large saucepan for about ten minutes or until tomatoes are soft.
2. Cool and sieve or purée in an electric blender.
3. Sauté the garlic in the oil for five minutes.
4. Add celery, carrot, sugar, basil, parsley and tomato purée. Season to taste with salt and pepper.
5. Cook, uncovered, over a low heat for about 1½ hours, stirring occasionally.

Anchovy Sauce
(Salsa Acciughe)

⅛ lb (60 g) canned anchovy fillets
3 tablespoons olive oil
1 onion, chopped
2 cups canned tomatoes
salt and pepper

1. Drain the oil from the canned anchovies and mix the oil with the olive oil in the saucepan. Add onion and sauté until golden brown.
2. Add anchovies and mash to a paste.
3. Stir in tomatoes and cook, uncovered, over a low heat for about one hour, stirring occasionally.

Walnut Sauce
(Salsa di Noci)

½ lb (250 g) ground walnuts
1 clove garlic, crushed
½ teaspoon marjoram
½ cup (125 ml) olive oil
½ cup (125 ml) cream

1. Mix together the walnuts, garlic and marjoram.
2. Stir in the olive oil and then the cream. Mix thoroughly.

Anchovy Wine Sauce
(Salsa di Acciughe e Vino)

⅛ lb (60 g) canned anchovy fillets
1 clove garlic, crushed
¼ cup (62.5 ml) dry sherry
2 tablespoons chopped parsley

1. Sauté garlic in the oil from the anchovy can for three minutes.
2. Add anchovies and mash to a paste.
3. Add sherry and bring to boiling point. Remove from heat and add parsley. Mix well.

Barbecue Sauce
(Salsa per Arrostiti)

½ onion, minced
3 tablespoons wine vinegar
2 tablespoons sugar
½ cup (125 ml) water
1 cup tomato sauce
3 tablespoons Worcestershire
sauce

Combine all ingredients in a saucepan and simmer for ten minutes.

Meat Sauce
(Sugo di Carne)

1 cup dried mushrooms
¼ cup (62.5 g) butter
  or margarine
½ cup (125 ml) olive oil
½ lb (250 g) ground beef
3 slices bacon, chopped
1 carrot, chopped
1 stalk celery, chopped
2 small onions, chopped

1 cup (250 ml) red wine
salt and pepper
1 tablespoon flour
½ lb (250 g) ripe tomatoes,
  peeled and chopped
1 bay leaf
1 teaspoon thyme
2 cloves

1. Soak the mushrooms in warm water for about ½ hour. Drain and chop.
2. Combine half the butter or margarine and all the olive oil in a large saucepan. Brown the meat and bacon.
3. Add the carrot, celery and onions and cook for ten minutes.
4. Add the wine, salt and pepper and cook until wine has evaporated.
5. Mix the remaining butter or margarine with the flour and add to the sauce, stirring well.
6. Add the tomatoes, bay leaf, thyme and cloves. Pour on enough water to cover, cover the saucepan with a lid and simmer for one hour. Before serving remove bay leaf and cloves.

Meat

Ossobuco

8 veal shanks
½ cup flour
salt and pepper
¾ cup (186 g) butter or margarine
¾ cup (186 ml) dry white wine
8 large tomatoes, peeled and chopped
2 cloves garlic, crushed
1½ teaspoons grated lemon rind
3 tablespoons chopped parsley

1. Roll the shanks in the flour seasoned with salt and pepper.
2. Melt the butter in a large saucepan and brown the shanks on all sides.
3. Add the wine and cook over a low heat for ten minutes.
4. Add the tomatoes and the garlic, cover and simmer for about 1½ hours.
5. Before serving sprinkle with grated rind and chopped parsley.

Serves 4-8.

Pot Roast
(Fetta di Manzo)

2 lb (1 kg) chuck roast in one piece	1 clove garlic
¼ cup (62.5 ml) butter	2½ cups canned tomatoes
¼ cup (62.5 ml) olive oil	1 bay leaf
	salt and pepper

1. Brown the garlic in the butter and oil for about two minutes.
2. Remove the garlic and brown the meat on all sides for ten minutes.
3. Add tomatoes, bay leaf and salt and pepper to taste.
4. Cover saucepan tightly and simmer for about 2½-3 hours or until meat is tender. Add a little beef stock if too dry.

Serves 4-6.

Sicilian Steak
(Bistecca alla Siciliana)

4 pieces of steak of your choice
2 cloves garlic, crushed
½ cup (125 ml) olive oil
3 tablespoons grated Parmesan cheese
1 cup (110 g) bread crumbs
salt and pepper

1. Mix together the garlic and the oil.
2. Dip steaks in the mixture.
3. Combine the grated cheese, bread crumbs and salt and pepper. Coat steaks with this mixture.
4. Cook steaks under a hot broiler, turning once.

Serves 4.

Beef in Red Wine (Carbonata)

4 pieces of rump steak
4 tablespoons (80 g) butter
  or margarine
4 onions, sliced
3 tablespoons flour

½ bottle dry red wine
salt and pepper
marjoram
nutmeg

1. Brown the steaks in the butter or margarine. Put in a flameproof casserole dish.
2. Sauté the onion in the same fat until transparent. Sprinkle the flour over the onions and continue cooking until golden brown.
3. Spread the onions over the meat, pour on the red wine, season with salt, pepper, marjoram and nutmeg.
4. Cook over a medium heat for about 30 minutes.

Serves 4.

Beef Stew (Stufato di Manzo)

3 lb (1½ kg) chuck roast
2 tablespoons olive oil
½ lb (250 g) bacon, chopped
1 large onion, sliced
2 cloves garlic, crushed
salt and pepper
¼ teaspoon marjoram

¼ teaspoon rosemary
½ cup (125 ml) red wine
4 tablespoons tomato paste
½ cup (125 ml) water
½ lb (250 g) button mushrooms
½ lb (250 g) small onions

1. Cut roast into bite-size pieces.
2. Heat the oil in a large saucepan. Add the bacon, onion and garlic and sauté until golden brown.
3. Season meat with salt, pepper, marjoram and rosemary. Add to saucepan and brown well on all sides.
4. Add red wine and tomato paste mixed with ½ cup water. Mix well.
5. Add enough boiling water to cover meat. Cover saucepan and simmer for about 2½ hours or until meat is tender. A half hour before the meat is cooked, stir in the mushrooms and onions.

Serves 6-8.

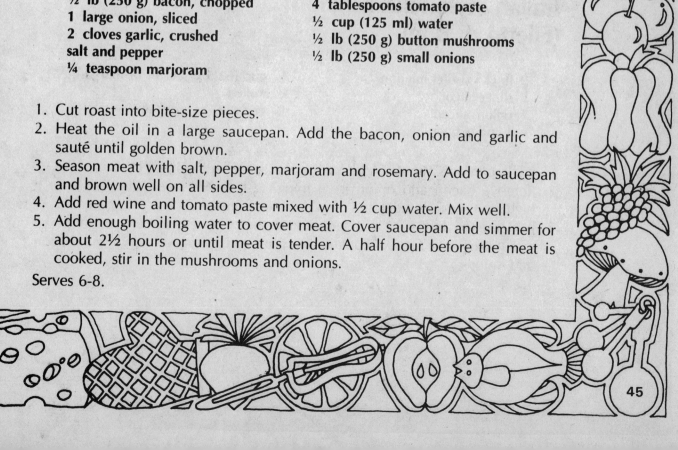

Rolled Meat Loaf
(Polpettone)

2 lb (1 kg) ground lean beef	¼ lb (125 g) Mozzarella cheese, sliced
2 tablespoons chopped parsley	4 tablespoons olive oil
1 teaspoon salt	1 cup (250 g) tomato paste
¼ teaspoon pepper	1 cup (250 ml) water
4 slices ham	bay leaf
1 cup mashed potatoes	

1. Mix together the meat, parsley, salt and pepper.
2. Turn meat mixture onto a floured board and flatten meat out to a rectangular shape.
3. Put ham slices on the meat, then spread on the mashed potatoes and lay the slices of Mozzarella on top. Roll up like a jelly roll and press edges closed.
4. Heat two tablespoons of olive oil in a large frypan. Place meat loaf in pan and pour remaining oil over the meat.
5. Cover frypan and simmer for about 15 minutes.
6. Mix tomato paste with the water and bay leaf. Pour over the meat, cover and simmer for about one hour. Remove loaf from frypan and allow to stand for about ten minutes before slicing.

Serves 4.

Italian Style Filet Mignon
(Filetto di Bue)

2 lb (1 kg) filet mignon	¼ cup (62.5 g) butter or margarine, melted
3 slices bacon	½ cup (125 ml) dry sherry
1 onion, sliced	
salt and pepper	

1. Fry bacon one minute. Add onions and sauté until golden brown.
2. Remove bacon and onion from frypan. Brown meat on all sides over a high heat. Reduce heat and cook for five minutes.
3. Add melted butter or margarine and sherry and cook for another two minutes or until meat is cooked. Do not overcook meat. Serve with bacon and onions.

Serves 6.

Steak with Garlic and Tomatoes
(Bistecca alla Pizzaiola)

¼ cup (62.5 ml) olive oil
1 garlic clove, crushed
1½ lb (750 g) tomatoes, peeled
   and chopped

1 teaspoon oregano
1 teaspoon salt
pepper
6 sirloin steaks

1. Sauté the garlic in half the oil for two minutes.
2. Stir in the tomatoes, oregano, salt and pepper. Cook, stirring constantly, for five minutes. Remove from heat.
3. Brown the steaks well on both sides in the remaining oil.
4. Reduce heat, spread tomato and garlic mixture over the steaks, cover and cook for about ten minutes.

Serves 6.

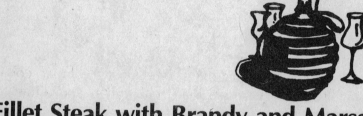

Fillet Steak with Brandy and Marsala
(Filetto Casanova)

4 pieces fillet steak
salt and pepper
olive oil
2 tablespoons (40 g) butter
   or margarine

2 lb (125 g) liver paté
¼ cup (62.5 ml) Marsala
⅓ cup (83 ml) brandy

1. Rub the steaks with salt and pepper and then with a little olive oil. Allow to stand for about an hour.
2. Brown the steaks either in a frypan or under a broiler for about one minute on each side.
3. Melt the butter in a large frypan and mix in the liver paté. Add Marsala and blend thoroughly. Cook for one minute.
4. Add the steaks and cook for a couple of minutes.
5. Warm the brandy and pour over the steaks. Light the brandy and continue to cook the steaks until the flames go out.

Serves 4.

Roast Lamb
(Agnello al Forno)

4 lb (2 kg) leg of lamb
2 cloves garlic, sliced
fresh rosemary
salt and pepper

½ cup (125 ml) olive oil
4 onions, quartered
2 lb (1 kg) new potatoes

1. Make small cuts in the lamb and insert slices of garlic and bits of rosemary in the incisions.
2. Rub the meat with salt and pepper and brush with the oil.
3. Roast in a 400°F (200°C) oven for about 1½-2 hours.
4. Add the onions and potatoes to the roasting pan 30 minutes after commencement of cooking. Baste occasionally.

Serves 6-8.

Lamb Stew Peasant Style
(Agnello alla Paesana)

2 lb (1 kg) lean stewing
   lamb, cubed
¼ cup (62.5 ml) olive oil
1 clove garlic, chopped
4 anchovy fillets, chopped

1 onion, chopped
1 stalk celery, sliced
¼ teaspoon rosemary
1 cup (250 ml) white wine
salt and pepper

1. Brown the lamb in the olive oil on all sides. Remove from saucepan and keep warm.
2. Sauté the garlic in the same oil. (Add more, if necessary).
3. Add anchovies and mash to a paste.
4. Add onion and celery and cook for five minutes.
5. Return the lamb to the saucepan; add rosemary, wine and salt and pepper to taste.
6. Cover and cook over a medium heat for about 45 minutes or until lamb is tender. Add a little water if stew is too dry.

Serves 4-6.

Lamb with Peppers
(Agnello con Peperoni)

4 lb (2 kg) lean lamb,
   cubed
salt and pepper
½ cup flour
¼ cup (62.5 ml) olive oil
2 cloves garlic, crushed
1 cup (250 ml) dry white wine

1 cup (250 ml) water
2 green peppers, sliced
2 red peppers, sliced
½ lb (250 g) tomatoes, peeled
   and chopped
1 bay leaf
pinch of oregano

1. Toss the meat in the flour seasoned with salt and pepper.
2. Sauté the garlic in the oil for three minutes.
3. Add the meat and brown well.
4. Stir in the wine and water. Add the peppers, tomatoes, bay leaf and oregano.
5. Cover and cook over a medium heat for about one hour or until meat is tender.

Serves 8.

Neapolitan Lamb
(Agnello alla Napoletana)

4 lb (2 kg) leg of lamb, boned
3 slices of bacon
¼ cup (62.5 g) butter or margarine
2 cloves garlic, crushed
2 small onions, chopped

¼ cup chopped mint
1 cup (250 ml) water
2 tablespoons sherry
1 cup (250 ml) tomato purée

1. Put bacon slices inside the lamb, roll up and tie with string.
2. Sprinkle meat with salt and pepper.
3. Melt the butter or margarine in a large saucepan and brown the lamb on all sides. Remove from pan.
4. Sauté the garlic and onions in the same pan until golden brown.
5. Add mint, water, sherry and tomato purée and mix well.
6. Return lamb to saucepan, cover and simmer for about two hours or until meat is tender. Add more water, if necessary.

Lamb with Egg and Lemon Sauce (Agnello Brodettato)

2 tablespoons bacon fat
2 lb (1 kg) boneless lamb
   (cut into cubes)
salt and pepper
3 tablespoons flour
1 clove garlic, crushed

½ cup (125 ml) dry white wine
3 cups (750 ml) beef stock
1 bay leaf
3 egg yolks
1 tablespoon lemon juice
2 tablespoons chopped parsley

1. Melt the bacon fat in a frypan and brown the lamb, a few cubes at a time, until golden brown on all sides. Remove cubes to a flame-proof casserole dish. Reserve fat in the frypan.

2. Season lamb with salt and pepper and sprinkle with flour. Toss well until all cubes are coated. Place lamb in a 500°F (260°C) oven, uncovered for about ten minutes. Turn occasionally. Remove casserole from the oven and reduce heat to 350°F (180°C).

3. Sauté the garlic in the frypan for about one minute. Stir in the wine and boil for about two minutes.

4. Stir in the stock and the bay leaf and simmer for three minutes. Pour over the lamb.

5. Place casserole over a high heat on top of the stove and bring to a boil. Return to the oven and cook, covered, for about 45 minutes. Remove the lamb cubes to a heated serving dish.

6. Strain the gravy and skim off the fat.

7. Beat together the egg yolks and lemon juice. Add a little of the strained gravy and beat well. Beat the egg and lemon mixture into the gravy and cook, stirring constantly, over a low heat until thick. Pour over the lamb and garnish with chopped parsley.

Lamb Chops Parmesan
(Cotolette Parmigiano)

8 thick loin lamb chops
½ cup (60 g) grated Parmesan cheese
2 tablespoons (40 g) butter or margarine

1 teaspoon lemon juice
½ teaspoon oregano
½ teaspoon salt
¼ teaspoon pepper

1. Broil lamb chops on both sides.
2. Mix together the cheese, butter or margarine, lemon juice, oregano, salt and pepper.
3. Spread over the chops and return to the broiler. Cook until the cheese mixture is brown.

Serves 4.

Veal Scaloppine

1½ lb (750 g) veal cutlets, without bone
¼ cup flour
salt and pepper
½ cup (125 g) butter or margarine

2 teaspoons lemon juice
1 cup (250 ml) marsala or dry white wine

1. Flatten meat.
2. Mix together flour, salt and pepper. Coat meat with flour.
3. Melt butter or margarine in a frypan and brown veal over a high heat on both sides for about two minutes each side.
4. Mix together the lemon juice and wine and pour over the meat. Reduce heat, cover and cook for another two minutes. Do not boil.

Serves 4.

Veal Cutlets in White Wine
(Cotolette di Vitello in Vino Bianco)

8 veal cutlets
½ cup flour
salt and pepper
4 tablespoons (80 g) butter
  or margarine

2 slices bacon, chopped
½ teaspoon sage
½ teaspoon rosemary
1 cup (250 ml) dry white wine
pinch of salt

1. Coat the cutlets with the flour seasoned with salt and pepper.
2. Heat the butter or margarine and bacon in a frypan for two minutes. Add the cutlets sprinkled with the sage and rosemary and brown on both sides.
3. Add the wine and a pinch of salt, cover and cook over a low heat for about ½ hour. Turn the cutlets occasionally and baste with sauce.

Serves 4.

Veal Parmesan
(Vitello alla Parmigiana)

1½ lb (750 g) veal cutlets
¼ cup (62.5 g) butter or margarine
1 clove garlic, crushed
¼ lb (125 g) mushrooms, sliced

½ cup (125 ml) sherry
½ cup (60 g) grated Parmesan cheese
salt and pepper

1. Pound veal flat and brown on both sides in the butter or margarine over a high heat. Put veal into a baking dish and keep warm.
2. Sauté the garlic and mushrooms in the same pan as the veal over a low heat for 5-10 minutes.
3. Remove pan from the heat and add sherry, grated Parmesan cheese and salt and pepper to taste. Pour sauce over the veal cutlets.
4. Bake in a 325°F (160°C) oven until meat is tender.

Serves 4.

Veal with Ham
(Saltimbocca alla Romana)

2 lb (1 kg) veal steak,
  thinly sliced
10 slices prosciutto
1 teaspoon sage

pepper
½ cup (125 g) butter or margarine
½ cup (125 ml) Marsala or
  dry white wine

1. Flatten veal.
2. Place slice of prosciutto on each piece of veal. Sprinkle with sage and pepper.
3. Roll up the veal and secure with a toothpick.
4. Melt butter or margarine in a frypan and cook the veal on all sides until golden brown, about ten minutes. Remove from pan and keep warm.
5. Add wine to the scraping in the frypan, heat and pour over the veal.

Serves 4-6.

Baked Veal Cutlets
(Vitello Imbottito al Forno)

1½ lb (750 g) veal cutlets
1 cup (250 ml) olive oil
1 cup (125 g) bread crumbs
salt and pepper

3 tablespoons grated Parmesan
  cheese
3 onions, sliced
1½ lb (750 g) tomatoes, peeled

1. Dip cutlets in the oil.
2. Mix together the bread crumbs, salt, pepper and cheese. Coat the cutlets with this mixture.
3. Grease a baking dish with the oil and put half the sliced onions on the bottom of the dish.
4. Arrange the veal on top of the onions.
5. Mash the tomatoes and spread over the veal.
6. Top with the remaining onions.
7. Bake in a 375°F (190°C) oven for about 30 minutes or until meat is tender.

Serves 4.

Veal Cutlets Milanese
(Cotolette alla Milanese)

1½ lb (750 g) veal cutlets	1 cup (125 g) bread crumbs
½ cup flour	¼ cup (62.5 g) butter or
2 egg yolks	margarine
salt and pepper	lemon wedges

1. Gently pound the cutlets thin. Roll in flour.
2. Beat egg yolks with salt and pepper. Dip the cutlets in the egg yolks and roll in bread crumbs.
3. Fry cutlets in the butter or margarine until golden brown.
4. Serve with lemon wedges.

Serves 4.

Veal Florentine
(Vitello alla Fiorentina)

2 lb (1 kg) veal steak, cubed	½ lb (250 g) tomatoes, peeled
1 onion, sliced	pinch of rosemary
¼ cup (62.5 ml) olive oil	¼ cup (62.5 ml) dry white wine
1 clove garlic, crushed	salt and pepper

1. Sauté the onion in the oil for about two minutes. Add garlic and cook for another minute.
2. Add meat and brown well on all sides.
3. Add tomatoes, rosemary, wine and salt and pepper to taste. Cover and cook over a low heat for about 30 minutes or until meat is tender. Stir occasionally.

Serves 6.

Veal with Anchovies and Tuna
(Vitello con Acciughe e Tonno)

2 lb (1 kg) veal, in one piece
1 cup (250 ml) dry white wine
1 onion, chopped
1 carrot, chopped
1 stalk celery, chopped
1 bay leaf
salt and pepper

½ lb (250 g) canned tuna fish
3 anchovy fillets
2 egg yolks
¼ cup (62.5 ml) olive oil
juice of one lemon
1 tablespoon capers

1. Place veal in a large saucepan with the wine, onion, carrot, celery, bay leaf and salt and pepper to taste. Slowly bring to a boil. Reduce heat and cook, covered, until the veal is tender, about 1½ hours.
2. Remove meat from the broth, drain and pat dry.
3. Mash together the tuna fish and the anchovy fillets. Rub through a fine sieve.
4. Add the egg yolks to the paste and then add the olive oil, lemon juice and capers.
5. Cut the veal into thin slices and spread with the tuna fish and anchovy paste. Cover and chill for several hours before serving.

Serves 6.

Veal Mozzarella
(Vitello alla Mozzarella)

6 slices veal steak
3 eggs
1 cup (125 g) bread crumbs
2 tablespoons chopped parsley
3 tablespoons grated Romano
   cheese
salt and pepper
⅓ cup (83 ml) olive oil
Tomato Sauce
6 slices Mozzarella cheese

1. Beat eggs slightly.
2. Combine bread crumbs, parsley, grated cheese, salt and pepper.
3. Dip veal in eggs and roll in bread crumbs.
4. Heat oil in a frypan and brown veal on both sides.
5. Put into a baking dish. Pour over Tomato Sauce. Place one slice of Mozzarella cheese on top of each piece of veal.
6. Bake in a 275°F (140°C) oven for about 20 minutes.

Serves 4-6.

Tomato Sauce

½ cup (125 ml) olive oil
1 onion, chopped
6 oz (185 g) tomato paste
2 lb (1 kg) tomatoes, peeled
3 cups (750 ml) water
salt and pepper
1 bay leaf
1 teaspoon oregano

1. Heat oil in a saucepan and saute the onion until transparent.
2. Add tomato paste, tomatoes and water and mix well.
3. Add salt, pepper, bay leaf and oregano and cook, uncovered, for about one hour over a low heat.

Chicken Cacciatore (Pollo alla Cacciatore)

4 lb (2 kg) chicken pieces
flour seasoned with salt and pepper
½ cup (125 ml) oil
2 onions, minced
1 green pepper, chopped
1 clove garlic, crushed
4 cups canned tomatoes

½ cup (125 ml) tomato purée
3 tablespoons tomato paste
2 teaspoons salt
½ teaspoon black pepper
1 teaspoon thyme
½ teaspoon mixed spice
½ cup (125 ml) light red wine

1. Toss chicken pieces in the seasoned flour. Brown in the hot oil.
2. Add onions, green pepper and garlic and cook for ten minutes.
3. Add tomatoes, tomato purée mixed with tomato paste, salt, pepper, thyme and mixed spice and cook, uncovered, for 15-20 minutes.
4. Add the wine, cover and cook for about 45 minutes or until chicken is tender.

Serves 6-8.

Chicken with Egg and Lemon Sauce (Pollo con Uova e Limone)

1 onion, chopped
1 tablespoon chopped parsley
2 tablespoons (40 g) butter or
margarine
4 chicken breasts, cut in half
flour seasoned with salt
and pepper

2 tablespoons chopped fennel
1½ cups (375 ml) chicken stock
1 lb (500 g) shelled peas
2 chicken livers, chopped
2 egg yolks
2 tablespoons lemon juice
salt and pepper

1. Sauté the onion and parsley in the butter or margarine for three minutes.
2. Coat chicken with seasoned flour and brown in fry pan with the onion and parsley.
3. Add the fennel and chicken stock, cover and simmer for about ½ hour.
4. In another saucepan, cook the peas in boiling salted water until just tender. Drain and add to the chicken with the chicken livers. Cook for another 15 minutes.
5. Combine the egg yolks with lemon juice. Remove the chicken from the heat and stir in the egg yolks and lemon juice. Season to taste with salt and pepper and serve immediately.

Serves 4-6.

Chicken with Spaghetti (Pollo Tetrazzini)

3 tablespoons (60 g) butter
  or margarine
2 tablespoons flour
2 cups (500 ml) chicken stock
salt and pepper to taste
1 cup (250 ml) cream

3 tablespoons sherry
½ lb (250 g) spaghetti
3 cups diced chicken
3 tablespoons whipped cream
grated Parmesan cheese

1. Melt the butter or margarine in a saucepan. Stir in the flour. Gradually add the chicken stock, stirring constantly. Season to taste with salt and pepper. Remove from heat and add the cream and sherry.
2. Cook spaghetti in boiling salted water until tender. Drain.
3. Add half the sauce to the spaghetti. Mix the other half with the chicken.
4. Put the spaghetti in a well-buttered baking dish. Place the chicken in the center. Spread whipped cream on top and sprinkle with Parmesan cheese.
5. Bake in a 375°F (190°C) oven for about 30 minutes or until heated thoroughly.

Serves 4-6.

Chicken with Basil (Pollo con Basilico)

½ cup (125 g) butter or
  margarine
3 onions, chopped
2 tablespoons chopped parsley
3 lb (1½ kg) chicken pieces
1 cup (250 ml) water

¼ lb (125 g) mushrooms, sliced
3 tablespoons fresh basil, minced
1 teaspoon dried rosemary
1 bay leaf
salt and pepper
½ cup (125 ml) dry white wine

1. In a large frypan, sauté the onions in the butter or margarine until transparent. Add parsley and cook for another three minutes.
2. Sauté the chicken pieces until golden brown.
3. Add water, mushrooms, basil, rosemary, bay leaf and salt and pepper to taste.
4. Cover and simmer over a low heat for about twenty minutes.
5. Add wine and cook for another twenty minutes or until chicken is tender.
Serves 4-6.

Chicken with Brandy (Pollo con Liquore)

8 chicken pieces
½ cup (125 g) butter or margarine
1 onion, chopped
3 tablespoons brandy

6 tablespoons flour
⅓ cup (83 ml) cream
2 cups (500 ml) chicken stock
salt and pepper
pinch nutmeg

1. Sauté the chicken pieces in two tablespoons of the butter or margarine. When brown all over, reduce heat and cook for ½ hour.
2. In a separate frypan, sauté the onion in two tablespoons butter or margarine until transparent. Remove from heat and stir in the brandy.
3. Pour over the chicken and cook over a low heat for ten minutes.
4. Melt remaining butter or margarine in a small saucepan. Stir in the flour and gradually add the cream and stock, stirring constantly. Cook over a low heat until thick and smooth.
5. Pour the white sauce over the chicken and stir.

Serves 4-8.

Duck Stuffed with Sausage (Anitra Imbottita)

1 duck (about 4 lb)
½ lb (250 g) Italian sausage, chopped
1 cup cooked rice

½ cup (60 g) bread crumbs
1 egg
2 tablespoons chopped parsley

1. Wash duck with cold water, drain and pat dry.
2. Mix together the sausage, rice, bread crumbs, egg and parsley.
3. Stuff duck with the mixture.
4. Bake in a 325°F (160°C) oven for about 1½ hours. Baste occasionally with drippings.

Serves 4.

Italian Duck
(Anitra con Liquore)

1 clove garlic	2 teaspoons salt
4 tablespoons (80 g) butter or margarine	½ teaspoon black pepper
	½ cup (125 ml) brandy
4 lb (2 kg) duck, cut into pieces	1 cup (250 ml) dry white wine
	½ lb (250 g) mushrooms, sliced
1 can Italian peeled tomatoes	½ lb (250 g) large green olives, sliced
2 tablespoons chopped parsley	
1 bay leaf	
½ teaspoon thyme	

1. Sauté the clove of garlic in the butter for two minutes.
2. Remove the garlic and sauté the duck pieces over a medium heat for ten minutes, turning the pieces occasionally.
3. Add tomatoes, parsley, bay leaf, thyme, salt and pepper. Cover and simmer over a low heat for 30-40 minutes.
4. Add brandy and white wine and continue to cook, uncovered, for twenty minutes.
5. Stir in mushrooms and olives and cook for another 20-30 minutes.
6. Before serving, skim the fat from the sauce.

Serves 4.

Duck with Olives
(Anitra alle Olive)

5 lb (2½ kg) duck	1 carrot, chopped
salt and pepper	1 tablespoon chopped parsley
sage and thyme to taste	
1 bay leaf	1 cup (250 ml) red wine
2 tablespoons olive oil	½ lb (250 g) black olives, pitted and sliced
1 onion, chopped	

1. Rub salt, pepper, sage and thyme on the inside of the duck. Add bay leaf. Brown the duck in the oil. Remove from the frypan.
2. Sauté the onion, carrot and parsley in the frypan for three minutes.
3. Return the duck, stir in the wine and cover. Cook over a low heat for about 1-1½ hours or until duck is tender.
4. Remove duck, add olives and cook for three minutes. Serve duck cut into pieces with the sauce poured over.

Serves 4-5.

Roast Pork
(Maiale Arrosto)

4 lb (2 kg) loin of pork
4 garlic cloves, sliced
½ onion, minced
2 tablespoons olive oil
pinch of marjoram

rosemary leaves
salt and pepper
1 teaspoon crushed bay leaf
water

1. Remove the rind and half the fat from the loin.
2. Make good sized incisions into the loin and insert a slice of garlic, minced onion mixed with oil and marjoram and a couple of rosemary leaves.
3. Rub the meat with salt and pepper and sprinkle with crushed bay leaf.
4. Place loin in a baking dish and pour a little water in the bottom of the pan.
5. Bake in a 375°F (190°C) oven for about 2½ hours.

Serves 6.

Pork chops with Wine
(Cotolette di Maiale al Vino Rosso)

8 pork chops
2 tablespoons (40 g) butter
   or margarine
2 tablespoons lemon juice

salt and pepper
1 cup (250 ml) red wine
   (Chianti if possible)

1. Melt butter or margarine in a large frypan.
2. Dip the chops into the lemon juice and rub generously with salt and pepper.
3. Brown the chops in the butter or margarine on both sides.
4. Pour the wine over the chops and simmer until chops are tender. Turn the chops occasionally.
5. Serve with wine sauce poured over the chops.

Serves 4-8.

61

Rabbit Stew
(Coniglio Stufato)

4 lb (2 kg) rabbit, cut into pieces
3 tablespoons olive oil
5 slices bacon, chopped
2 onions, chopped
2 cloves garlic, crushed
3 tablespoons chopped parsley

1 tablespoon fresh chopped
   basil
1 bay leaf
salt and pepper
1 cup (250 ml) dry red wine

1. Soak the rabbit pieces in cold salted water for two hours. Drain and dry.
2. Heat the oil in a large saucepan. Sauté the rabbit, bacon, onions, garlic and parsley for about ½ hour.
3. Add the basil, bay leaf, salt and pepper to taste and wine.
4. Cover and cook over a low heat for another ½ hour or until rabbit is tender.

Serves 6.

Fried Rabbit
(Coniglio Fritto)

1 rabbit
2 tablespoons lemon juice
salt and pepper
½ lb (250 g) bacon
3 tablespoons olive oil

1. Cut the rabbit into pieces and soak in cold salted water for two hours. Drain and dry thoroughly.
2. Mix lemon juice with salt and pepper and rub onto each rabbit piece.
3. Chop bacon and fry in the oil until crisp. Remove the bacon.
4. Put rabbit pieces in the frypan and cook until tender. Just before the end of the cooking, return the bacon pieces.

Serves 2-3.

Kidneys with Lemon
(Rognoni di Vitello Trifolati)

4 veal kidneys
¼ cup (62.5 ml) olive oil
salt and pepper
2 tablespoons parsley
juice of one lemon

1. Remove the fat and membranes from the kidneys and slice thinly. Soak in cold salted water for one hour. Rinse well and dry.
2. Heat the oil in a frypan, add the sliced kidneys and cook quickly over a high heat, stirring constantly.
3. Add salt and pepper, parsley and lemon juice. Reduce heat and cook for another minute.

Serves 4.

Kidneys with Mushrooms
(Rognoni con Funghi)

4 veal kidneys
1 lb (500 g) button mushrooms
4 tablespoons olive oil
salt and pepper

1. Remove fat and membranes from the kidneys. Slice in ½ inch (1-cm) slices and soak in cold salted water for ten minutes. Rinse, drain and dry.
2. Wipe the mushrooms with a damp cloth and sauté with the kidneys in the oil over a low heat for about seven minutes. Stir occasionally.

Serves 4.

Liver Milanese
(Fegato alla Milanese)

1 lb (500 g) beef liver, ½-inch (1-cm) slices
salt and pepper
4 tablespoons flour
¼ cup (62.5 ml) olive oil

1 onion, sliced
½ lb (250 g) mushrooms, sliced
2 tablespoons tomato paste
¼ cup (62.5 ml) red wine

1. Dredge liver in seasoned flour.
2. Heat oil in a frypan and brown liver on both sides over a high heat for about two minutes each side. Remove from pan and keep warm.
3. Sauté the onion and mushrooms in the same oil.
4. Mix the tomato paste with the red wine and add to the onion and mushroom mixture. Cook for 5 minutes.
5. Return the liver to the pan and cook for another two minutes.

Serves 4.

Fried Liver
(Fegato Fritto)

1 lb (500 g) liver, thinly sliced
1 egg, beaten
¼ cup bread crumbs
salt and pepper
3 tablespoons olive oil
lemon wedges

1. Dip the liver slices in the beaten egg.
2. Coat with bread crumbs mixed with salt and pepper.
3. Fry the liver in the oil over a high heat for one minute on each side. Reduce heat and cook for another three minutes.
4. Serve garnished with lemon wedges.

Serves 4.

Liver and Onions
(Fegato alla Veneziana)

1 lb (500 g) calves' liver, sliced thin	2 onions, sliced
3 tablespoons (60 g) butter or margarine	½ cup (125 ml) dry white wine
	1 tablespoon chopped parsley
	salt and pepper

1. Sauté the onions in the butter or margarine for about three minutes.
2. Add the liver and brown on both sides over a high heat.
3. Add wine and simmer for five minutes.
4. Remove from heat, sprinkle with parsley, salt and pepper.

Serves 4.

Sweet and Sour Liver
(Fegato Dolce e Agro)

1 lb (500 g) liver, sliced
salt and pepper
2 tablespoons olive oil
Sweet and Sour Sauce

1. Season liver with salt and pepper.
2. Heat oil in a frypan and sauté the liver over a high heat for about two minutes. Reduce heat and cook for another two minutes.
3. Cover with Sweet and Sour Sauce and cook for one more minute or until liver is tender.

Serves 4.

Sweet and Sour Sauce

4 tablespoons olive oil
2 onions, sliced
1 teaspoon brown sugar
2 tablespoons wine vinegar
salt and pepper

Sauté onions in oil until transparent. Add remaining ingredients and heat thoroughly.

Fish Fillets in White Wine
(Filetti di Pesce al Vino Bianco)

2 lb (1 kg) fish fillets (of
    your choice)
butter or margarine
2 tablespoons lemon juice

1 tablespoon chopped parsley
1 tablespoon capers
½ cup (125 ml) white wine

1. Heat the butter or margarine in a large frypan.
2. Add the fish, lemon juice, parsley and capers. Cover and cook for ten minutes.
3. Turn the fish, add the wine and cook, uncovered, for about seven minutes.

Serves 4-6.

Flounder in Mushroom and Cream Sauce
(Passerino in Salsa di Funghi)

2 lb (1 kg) flounder fillets
4 cups (1 liter) fish stock
⅓ cup (83 g) butter or
    margarine
½ lb (250 g) mushrooms, sliced

¼ cup flour
¼ cup (30 g) grated Parmesan
    cheese
1 cup (250 ml) cream
salt and pepper

1. Cook the fish in the stock until just tender. Remove and keep warm.
2. Sauté the mushrooms in half the butter or margarine for five minutes.
3. Mix the other half of the butter or margarine with the flour and add to the simmering stock, stirring constantly. Cook until thick. Remove from heat and stir in the cheese and the cream. Season to taste with salt and pepper.
4. Place the fish on the bottom of a buttered baking dish. Spread the mushrooms over the fish and pour the white sauce over it all.
5. Bake in a 350°F (180°C) oven for about 20 minutes.

Serves 6.

Shrimp Risotto
(Risotto di Scampi)

2 tablespoons (40 g) butter or margarine	5 cups (1.2 liters) chicken stock
1 large onion, chopped	salt and pepper
1 clove garlic, crushed	⅛ lb (60 g) button mushrooms, sliced
1 cup (200 g) long grain rice	½ lb (250 g) shrimp, peeled
½ cup (125 ml) dry white wine	Parmesan cheese

1. Melt the butter or margarine in a saucepan and sauté the onion and garlic for about five minutes or until the onion is transparent.
2. Add the rice and continue cooking until the grains are golden.
3. Stir in the wine and boil until wine is reduced by half.
4. Stir in one cup of stock, salt and pepper to taste and the mushrooms. Cook uncovered until the stock has been absorbed. Continue adding the stock in one cup amounts until it has all been used. Add the shrimp with the last cup of stock. Garnish with Parmesan cheese.

Serves 4-6.

Broiled Garlic Shrimp
(Scampi all'Aglio)

1 lb (500 g) large shrimp	1 garlic, crushed
¼ cup (62.5 g) butter or margarine	½ teaspoon salt
3 tablespoons olive oil	¼ teaspoon black pepper
1½ teaspoons lemon juice	2 tablespoons chopped parsley
1 scallion, finely chopped	lemon wedges

1. Shell, de-vein and quickly wash and dry the shrimp.
2. Melt the butter or margarine in a large shallow baking dish. (It must be able to fit under the broiler).
3. Add the olive oil, lemon juice, scallion, garlic, salt and pepper.
4. Add the shrimp and turn them over in the mixture until they are completely coated on all sides.
5. Place under a very hot broiler. If the shrimp are uncooked, cook them for about five minutes on one side, then turn and cook for another five to ten minutes. If the shrimp are cooked, they must be thoroughly heated.
6. Serve garnished with chopped parsley and lemon wedges.

Serves 2.

Vegetables

Spinach Supreme

4 lb (2 kg) spinach
½ cup (125 ml) olive oil
2 cloves garlic, crushed
2 tablespoons chopped raisins
1 tablespoon pine nuts
6 anchovy fillets, chopped
10 green olives, pitted and chopped
10 black olives, pitted and chopped
1 tablespoon capers
1 tablespoon chopped basil

1. Wash the spinach very well and remove center white stem. Cook in a covered saucepan for five minutes. (Do not add any water.)
2. Drain the spinach and chop well.
3. Sauté the garlic in the olive oil until golden brown.
4. Add the raisins, pine nuts, anchovy fillets, olives, capers and basil and mix well.
5. Mix in the spinach and heat thoroughly.

Serves 6.

Breaded Eggplant
(Melanzana Impanata)

1 large eggplant
1 tablespoon salt
2 eggs, beaten
1 cup (110 g) bread crumbs
¼ cup (30 g) grated Parmesan
  cheese

⅛ teaspoon pepper
1 teaspoon basil
oil for deep frying

1. Cut eggplant into slices. (Do not peel.) Sprinkle salt on each slice. Put on a plate and put a weighted plate on top of the slices. Let stand for about one hour. Drain and pat dry.
2. Dip each slice in eggs, then dredge in bread crumbs mixed with cheese, pepper and basil.
3. Fry eggplant slices in oil until golden brown. Drain and serve immediately.

Serves 4.

Mushrooms in Wine
(Funghi con Vino)

1 lb (500 g) fresh button
  mushrooms
¼ cup (62.5 ml) olive oil
1 large onion, sliced

1 clove garlic, crushed
salt and pepper
1 cup (250 ml) dry white wine

1. Wipe mushrooms with a damp cloth.
2. Heat oil in a large frypan and saute the onion and garlic until golden brown.
3. Add the mushrooms and saute for about seven minutes.
4. Pour on the wine and cook over a low heat for another three minutes.

Serves 4-6.

Broccoli in Wine
(Broccoli alla Romana)

2 lb (1 kg) broccoli
salt and pepper
½ cup (125 ml) olive oil
2 cloves garlic, crushed
2 cups (500 ml) dry white wine

1. Heat the oil in a large saucepan and sauté the garlic until it is golden brown.
2. Add the wine and the prepared broccoli, stalks down. Sprinkle with salt and pepper.
3. Cook, uncovered, until tender.
4. Remove the broccoli to a warm serving dish and reduce the wine to about ½ cup over a high heat. Pour over the broccoli.

Serves 6.

Baked Cauliflower
(Cavolfiore al Forno)

1 medium cauliflower
1 tablespoon olive oil
½ cup (55 g) bread crumbs
½ cup (60 g) grated Parmesan cheese
¼ cup (62.5 ml) olive oil

1. Cut cauliflower into flowerets. Put in saucepan with a small amount of boiling salted water. Boil for about five minutes. Drain.
2. Spread one tablespoon olive oil over the bottom of a baking dish. Arrange cauliflower in dish.
3. Mix together the bread crumbs and the grated cheese. Sprinkle over the cauliflower.
4. Pour the ¼ cup olive oil over the top.
5. Bake in a 350°F (180°C) oven for about 30 minutes.

Serves 6.

Asparagus Florentine
(Sparagio alla Fiorentina)

2　bunches of fresh asparagus
8　slices prosciutto
¼　cup (62.5 g) butter or
　　margarine
¼　cup (30 g) grated Parmesan
　　cheese

1. Snap off tough ends of asparagus and wash stalks very well.
2. Cook asparagus in boiling salted water until just tender. Drain.
3. Wrap one piece of prosciutto around a few stalks and fasten with a tooth-pick.
4. Butter the bottom of a baking dish and lay bundles of asparagus in the dish. Sprinkle with cheese.
5. Bake in a 400°F (200°C) oven for about 10 minutes.

Serves 4-6.

Broccoli Parmesan
(Broccoli alla Parmigiana)

2　lb (1 kg) broccoli
salt and pepper
¼　cup (62.5 g) butter or
　　margarine, melted
½　cup (60 g) grated Parmesan
　　cheese

1. Put broccoli in a saucepan with a small amount of water and the butter or margarine. Season with salt and pepper, cover and cook until just tender.
2. Drain but reserve the liquid. Put broccoli on a serving dish, pour pan juices over the broccoli and sprinkle with Parmesan cheese.

Serves 6.

Zucchini Pie
(Torta di Zucchini)

1 lb (500 g) zucchini, sliced
2 tablespoons (40 g) butter or margarine
1 medium onion, chopped
½ cup (30 g) fresh bread crumbs

½ cup (30 g) grated Parmesan cheese
salt and pepper
6 eggs, beaten
2 tablespoons (40 g) butter or margarine

1. Sauté the zucchini and onion in two tablespoons of butter or margarine for about ten minutes.
2. Mix together the zucchini, onion, bread crumbs, cheese, salt and pepper to taste and the eggs.
3. Melt butter or margarine in a large frypan. Pour in the zucchini and egg mixture and cook without stirring until the bottom is set. Put frypan under hot broiler to cook the top.

Serves 6.

Eggplant with Mozzarella Cheese
(Melanzane Mozzarella)

3 lb (1½ kg) eggplant
salt
olive oil
2 onions, chopped
1 clove garlic, crushed

2 lb (1 kg) tomatoes, chopped
thyme and oregano to taste
½ cup (60 g) grated Parmesan cheese
1 lb (500 g) Mozzarella cheese

1. Slice the eggplant and sprinkle with salt. Set aside for about one hour. Drain and pat dry. Sauté in olive oil, drain and place in a baking dish.
2. Sauté the onions and garlic in olive oil for two minutes. Add tomatoes, thyme and oregano. Simmer for ½ hour.
3. Pour tomato sauce over the eggplant and sprinkle with Parmesan cheese.
4. Slice the Mozzarella and arrange slices on top. Dot with butter or margarine and bake in a 325°F (160°C) oven for one hour.

Serves 6.

Stuffed Tomatoes
(Pomodoro Ripieno)

6 large tomatoes
6 anchovy fillets, chopped
1 cup (125 g) bread crumbs
3 tablespoons grated Parmesan cheese

¼ lb (125 g) Italian sausage, chopped
salt and pepper
⅓ cup (83 ml) olive oil
1 teaspoon oregano

1. Slice off top of tomatoes and remove seeds and pulp. Be careful not to break the skin of the tomatoes.
2. Mix together the anchovies, bread crumbs, cheese, sausage, salt and pepper to taste, olive oil and oregano.
3. Fill the tomatoes with the mixture. Place in an oiled baking dish.
4. Bake in a 350°F (180°C) oven for about ½ hour.

Serves 6.

Garlic Potatoes
(Patete all'Aglio)

4 lb (2 kg) potatoes
1 cup (250 ml) olive oil
3 cloves garlic, crushed
salt and pepper
1 teaspoon oregano

1. Peel and slice the potatoes.
2. Heat the oil in a flame-proof casserole dish. Sauté the garlic until golden brown.
3. Add the potatoes and toss thoroughly. Cook over a medium heat for ten minutes.
4. Bake, uncovered, in a 350°F (180°C) oven for about 45 minutes or until the potatoes are tender.

Serves 8.

Vegetable Casserole
(Vegetali al Forno)

1 eggplant, sliced	1 clove garlic, crushed
2 onions, sliced	salt and pepper
3 zucchini, sliced	½ lb (250 g) Mozzarella
2 green peppers, chopped	cheese, grated
6 tomatoes, peeled and sliced	2 tablespoons chopped basil
½ cup (125 ml) olive oil	

1. Place layers of the vegetables in an oiled baking dish.
2. Mix the garlic with the oil and sprinkle over the vegetables. Season to taste with salt and pepper.
3. Sprinkle with Mozzarella cheese and chopped basil.

Serves 4-6.

Stuffed Baked Peppers
(Peperoni Farciti alla Napoletana)

6 large green peppers	10 black olives, pitted and chopped
4 tablespoons olive oil	1 cup bread crumbs
2 cloves garlic, crushed	1 teaspoon oregano
6 ripe tomatoes, peeled and chopped	salt and pepper
2 tablespoons capers	½ cup (125 ml) olive oil
3 tablespoons raisins, chopped	

1. Cut off the tops of the peppers and scoop out seeds and pith.
2. Heat the oil in a large saucepan and sauté the garlic for two minutes. Stir in the tomatoes, cover and cook for ten minutes.
3. Add the capers, raisins, olives, bread crumbs, oregano and salt and pepper to taste. Mix well.
4. Fill the pepper with the stuffing and place in an oiled baking dish close together. Sprinkle with the ½ cup of olive oil.
5. Bake in a 350°F (180°C) oven for about one hour.

Serves 6.

Peas Parmesan
(Pisella alla Parmigiana)

2 lb (1 kg) fresh shelled peas
⅓ cup (83 ml) olive oil
5 scallions, finely chopped
¼ cup (62.5 ml) water
2 tablespoons chopped parsley

1 tablespoon chopped fresh basil
salt and pepper
½ cup (60 g) grated Parmesan
  cheese

1. Sauté the scallions in the oil for three minutes.
2. Mix in water, peas, parsley, basil and salt and pepper to taste.
3. Cover and cook for about 10 minutes or until peas are tender. Do not overcook.
4. Drain peas and put in a hot serving dish. Sprinkle with Parmesan cheese.

Serves 6-8.

Cabbage with Bacon
(Cavolo alla Casalinga)

1 cabbage
salt and pepper
6 slices bacon
2 small onions, chopped

1 tablespoon vinegar
2½ cups (625 ml) water
salt and pepper

1. Remove outer leaves and coarsely cut the cabbage.
2. Chop the bacon slices and cook until transparent in a large saucepan.
3. Add onions and sauté until golden brown.
4. Add the cabbage, vinegar, water and salt and pepper to taste. Mix well. Cover and cook for about 20 minutes. Drain before serving.

Serves 6.

Mushrooms with Anchovy Sauce (Funghi Trifolati)

2 lb (1 kg) mushrooms, sliced
⅓ cup (83 ml) olive oil
2 cloves garlic, crushed
salt and pepper
3 tablespoons (60 g) butter
   or margarine

8 anchovy fillets, chopped
3 tablespoons chopped parsley
juice of one lemon

1. Wipe mushrooms with a damp cloth.
2. Sauté the garlic in the oil for two minutes.
3. Add the mushrooms and salt and pepper to taste. Cover and cook for about ten minutes. Remove mushrooms from the frypan and keep warm.
4. Stir in the butter or margarine, chopped anchovy fillets, parsley and lemon juice. Mix well and cook for about five minutes, stirring constantly.
5. Pour sauce over mushrooms and serve immediately.

Serves 6.

Mushrooms in Cream (Funghi Coltivati alla Crema)

2 lb (1 kg) button mushrooms
½ cup (125 g) butter or margarine
1 clove garlic, halved
½ cup (125 ml) dry red wine

1½ cups (375 ml) cream
salt and pepper
nutmeg

1. Wipe the mushrooms with a damp cloth.
2. Melt the butter or margarine in a large frypan. Sauté the garlic for two minutes. Remove garlic.
3. Sauté the mushrooms for ten minutes.
4. Add the wine, mix well and cook over a high heat until half the wine has evaporated. Reduce the heat.
5. Add the cream, salt and pepper to taste and a pinch of nutmeg. Cook over a very low heat, stirring constantly, for five minutes.

Serves 6.

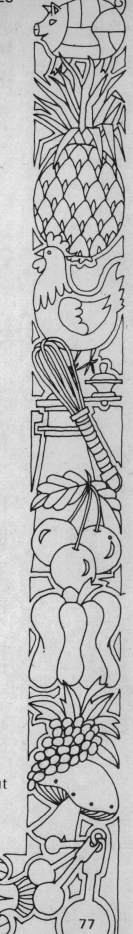

Stuffed Mushrooms
(Funghi Ripiene)

  1 lb (500 g) large fresh mushrooms
  ⅔ cup (85 g) bread crumbs
  salt and pepper
  ½ cup (60 g) grated Parmesan cheese
  ¼ teaspoon oregano
  ⅓ cup (83 ml) olive oil

1. Wipe the mushrooms with a damp cloth and remove stems.
2. Place mushrooms, top down, in a shallow baking dish.
3. Mix together bread crumbs, salt, pepper, cheese and oregano.
4. Fill mushroom tops with this mixture.
5. Sprinkle the oil over it all.
6. Bake in a 350°F (180°C) oven for about 15 minutes.

Serves 4.

Sauteed Mushrooms
(Funghi Fritti)

  1 lb (500 g) button mushrooms
  1 clove garlic, crushed
  4 tablespoons olive oil
  salt and pepper
  ¼ teaspoon oregano

1. Wipe the mushrooms with a damp cloth.
2. Saute the garlic in the oil for two minutes.
3. Add the mushrooms and seasonings and sauté over a low heat for about ten minutes.

Serves 4.

Potato Croquettes
(Crocchette di Patate)

2 lb (1 kg) potatoes	2 eggs, beaten
2 tablespoons (40 g) butter or margarine	salt and pepper
	pinch of nutmeg
½ cup (60 g) grated Parmesan cheese	one egg, beaten
	bread crumbs

1. Boil potatoes, drain and sieve through a fine strainer.
2. Add butter or margarine, cheese, beaten eggs, salt and pepper to taste and nutmeg.
3. Shape into croquettes. Dip in beaten egg and roll in bread crumbs.
4. Fry in oil until golden brown on all sides.

Serves 6.

Deep Fried Celery
(Sedano Fritto)

1 bunch celery	1 tablespoon olive oil
2 eggs	salt
¾ cup (186 ml) milk	oil for deep frying
8 tablespoons flour	

1. Wash the celery and cut into 3-inch (8-cm) lengths. Trim off coarse fibers.
2. Beat together the eggs and the milk.
3. Gradually add the flour and beat well.
4. Add the oil and 1 teaspoon salt. Mix thoroughly.
5. Cook the celery in boiling salted water for about 7 minutes. Drain and dry.
6. Dip the celery pieces in batter and fry in deep oil until golden brown. Drain and serve immediately.

Serves 6.

Eggs

Omelette with Ricotta Cheese
(Omelette con Ricotta)

8 eggs
2 tablespoons water
3 tablespoons (60 g) butter or margarine
1 small onion, minced
½ lb (250 g) Ricotta cheese
¼ cup (30 g) Parmesan cheese
2 tablespoons chopped parsley
salt and pepper

1. Beat the eggs lightly with the water.
2. Melt the butter or margarine in a large frypan and sauté the onion until golden brown.
3. Mix together the Ricotta and Parmesan cheese.
4. Pour the eggs into the frypan. Sprinkle cheese mixture and parsley over the eggs. Season to taste with salt and pepper.
5. Cover and cook over a low heat until eggs are set.

Serves 3-4.

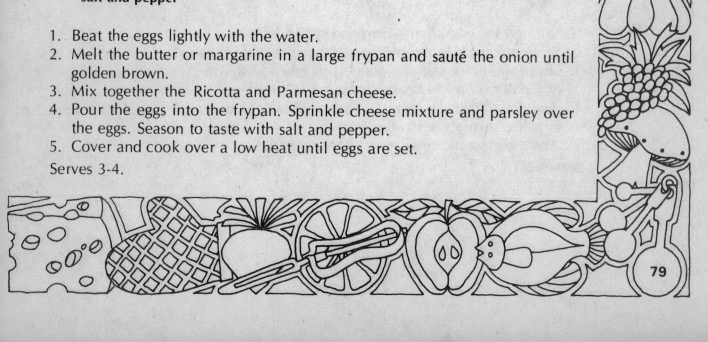

Cheese Omelette
(Frittata di Formaggio)

6 eggs
2 tablespoons water
¼ cup (62.5 ml) olive oil
¼ lb (125 g) Mozzarella cheese, diced
salt and pepper

1. Lightly beat the eggs with the water.
2. Heat the oil in a frypan and, stirring constantly, brown the cheese.
3. Add the eggs, season with salt and pepper and cook, covered, over a low heat until the bottom is browned and the eggs mostly set.
4. Put frypan under a very hot broiler to cook the top of the omelette.

Serves 2-3.

Sweet and Sour Eggs
(Uova in Salsa Agrodolce)

6 eggs
2 tablespoons (40 g) butter or margarine
2 small onions, minced
1 tablespoon flour
salt and pepper

1 cup (250 ml) chicken stock
3 cloves
1 bay leaf
1 tablespoon sugar
1 cup (250 ml) dry wine

1. Soft boil the eggs. Shell them and set aside.
2. Sauté the onion in the butter or margarine until transparent.
3. Stir in the flour, salt and pepper. Slowly add the stock, stirring constantly. Cook over a low heat for about five minutes.
4. Add the cloves, bay leaf, sugar and wine and cook for about ten minutes, stirring constantly.
5. Add the eggs and cook for another five minutes.

Serves 2-3.

Eggs with Zucchini
(Frittata di Zucchini)

6 eggs
2 tablespoons water
½ lb (250 g) zucchini
⅓ cup (83 g) butter or margarine

1 onion, minced
salt and pepper
¼ teaspoon marjoram
3 tomatoes, peeled and chopped

1. Beat the eggs lightly with the water.
2. Cut the zucchini into thin slices.
3. Saute the onion in the butter or margarine until golden brown.
4. Stir in the zucchini, salt and pepper to taste, marjoram and tomatoes. Cook until zucchini are tender.
5. Pour on the eggs, cover and cook at low heat until the eggs are set.

Serves 3.

Eggs with Anchovies
(Uova con Acciughe)

¼ cup (62.5 ml) olive oil
4 anchovy fillets
2 small onions, sliced
1 clove garlic, crushed
1 stalk celery, sliced
1 red pepper, chopped

½ lb (250 g) tomatoes, peeled,
    seeded and chopped
1½ cups (375 ml) water
salt and pepper
¼ teaspoon marjoram
12 eggs, hard boiled

1. Heat oil in a large saucepan. Add chopped anchovy fillets, onions, garlic, celery and red pepper. Sauté for ten minutes.
2. Add the tomatoes and water, cover and cook for 15 minutes. Season to taste with salt and pepper. Add marjoram.
3. Pour half the sauce in a serving dish. Slice the hard-boiled eggs and arrange on the sauce. Pour the remaining sauce over the eggs.

Serves 6-8.

Desserts & Cookies

Ricotta Cheese Pie
(Torta di Ricotta)

Pastry:
- ¾ cup sifted flour
- ½ teaspoon salt
- 1½ tablespoons (30 g) butter or margarine
- ¼ cup (62.5 g) lard
- 1 tablespoon sherry

Filling:
- ¾ lb (375 g) ricotta cheese
- 4 tablespoons flour
- ½ cup sugar
- 1 tablespoon lemon juice
- 2 eggs, separated
- ½ cup (125 ml) cream, whipped

1. To make the pastry, mix together the flour, salt, butter or margarine and lard until mixture is the consistency of coarse meal. Add sherry, a little at a time, until pastry forms a stiff ball. Chill. Roll out on a lightly floured board and line the bottom of a 9-inch (23-cm) pie pan.
2. Press ricotta cheese through a fine sieve. Add flour, sugar and lemon juice and mix well.
3. Beat egg yolks until thick and light-yellow colored. Gently mix into the ricotta mixture.
4. Fold the whipped cream into the mixture.
5. Beat the egg whites until stiff and gently fold into the ricotta mixture.
6. Pour into an unbaked pastry shell.
7. Bake in a 300°F (150°C) oven for one hour. Turn off the heat and leave the pie in the oven for another hour with the door closed. Remove from oven and cool.

Lady Fingers
(Savoiardi)

3 eggs, separated
1 teaspoon almond extract
¼ teaspoon salt

⅓ cup sugar
½ cup sifted cake flour
1 teaspoon baking powder

1. Beat egg yolks until thick and light-yellow colored. Beat in almond extract.
2. Beat egg whites until stiff. Continue beating, adding salt and sugar, until whites are glossy and very stiff.
3. Fold egg yolks into egg whites.
4. Fold in sifted flour and baking powder.
5. Drop batter by the tablespoon onto an ungreased cookie tin forming fingers about 1 x 3 inches (2½ x 8 cm).
6. Bake in a 350°F (180°C) oven for ten minutes. Remove from tray immediately and cool.

Makes about 3 dozen.

Sugar Cookies
(Pastini di Zucchero)

¾ cup (186 g) butter or
   margarine
1 cup sugar
1 egg
1 teaspoon vanilla

1 teaspoon baking powder
2¼ cups sifted flour
½ cup sugar
1 teaspoon cinnamon

1. Cream together butter or margarine and sugar until light and fluffy. Add egg and vanilla and beat well.
2. Sift together baking powder and flour and add to the creamed mixture. Blend well.
3. Shape dough into small balls and roll in the sugar mixed with the cinnamon. Place on a greased cookie tin.
4. Bake in a 400°F (200°C) oven for about ten minutes.

Makes about 3 dozen.

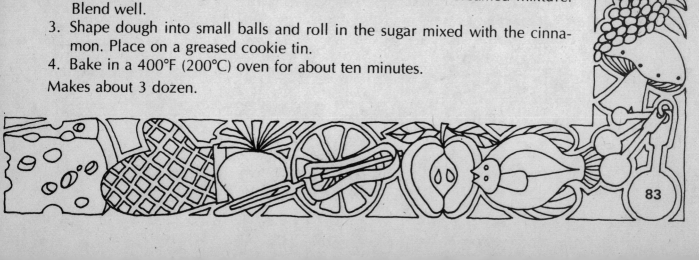

Christmas Cookies
(Pastini di Natale)

2½ cups sifted flour
pinch of salt
1 tablespoon baking powder
1 cup sugar
¼ cup (62.5 g) butter or
margarine
1 egg yolk, slightly beaten

1 teaspoon almond extract
½ cup (125 ml) milk
1 egg white
2 cups confectioners' sugar
1 cup (170 g) candied cherries
½ cup (60 g) chopped almonds

1. Sift together flour, salt, baking powder and sugar.
2. Mix in butter or margarine with fingers.
3. Add egg yolk, almond extract and milk. Mix to a firm ball. Turn onto a floured board and knead for about five minutes. Chill.
4. Roll out dough to a thickness of ¼-inch (5 mm). Cut into desired shapes and place on an ungreased cookie tin.
5. Beat egg white with sugar until foamy. Brush on each cookie. Decorate with candied cherries and chopped almonds.
6. Bake in a 375°F (190°C) oven for about ten minutes.

Makes about 4 dozen.

Rice Pudding
(Budino di Riso)

½ cup (105 g) uncooked rice
¼ cup sugar
3 eggs
4 cups (1 liter) milk
½ cup (80 g) raisins

¼ teaspoon nutmeg
¼ teaspoon salt
2 teaspoons lemon juice
2 teaspoons grated lemon rind

1. Pour rice into a well-buttered baking dish.
2. Mix together the sugar and eggs and beat well.
3. Add milk, raisins, nutmeg, salt, lemon juice and grated rind. Mix well.
4. Pour over the rice and stir. Dot with butter or margarine.
5. Bake in a 325°F (160°C) oven for about two hours. Mix several times during the first hour of cooking.

Serves 6-8.

Ricotta with Coffee
(Ricotta al Caffe)

1 lb (500 g) ricotta cheese
2 tablespoons finely ground coffee
½ cup sugar
⅓ cup (83 ml) rum

1. Beat ricotta until light and press through a fine sieve.
2. Add the coffee and sugar and mix well.
3. Add the rum and blend thoroughly.
4. Pour into a serving dish and chill for several hours.

Serves 4.

Rum Cake
(Dolce al Rum)

3 eggs	1 cup flour, sifted
1 cup sugar	2 teaspoons baking powder
¼ cup (62.5 ml) cold water	Topping
1½ teaspoons vanilla	

1. Beat eggs until light and lemon colored.
2. Slowly add the sugar, beating constantly.
3. Add water and vanilla and beat well.
4. Sift together flour and baking powder and fold into batter a little at a time.
5. Pour into a well-buttered and floured 9-inch (23-cm) cake pan.
6. Bake in a 350°F (180°C) oven for about 30 minutes. Cool in pan. Remove and spread topping over the cake.

Topping

1 tablespoon gelatin	4 egg yolks, lightly beaten
⅓ cup (83 ml) cold water	½ cup (125 ml) rum
1½ cups (375 ml) hot milk	1 cup chopped orange segments
¾ cup sugar	1 cup (250 ml) cream, whipped

1. Soak the gelatin in the cold water for five minutes.
2. Combine milk and sugar in a saucepan. When hot, add gelatin and dissolve.
3. Slowly pour gelatin and milk mixture over the egg yolks, stirring constantly. Add rum and mix well.
4. Place bowl over ice water and beat until thick.
5. Fold in orange segments and whipped cream and pour over cake.

Apricot Torte
(Torta di Albicocca)

6 eggs	1 teaspoon grated orange rind
1 cup sugar	1½ cups cake flour
1½ teaspoons grated lemon rind	Apricot Frosting

1. Beat eggs until light and lemon colored.
2. Slowly add the sugar beating constantly.
3. Add lemon and orange rinds and beat until thick.
4. Sift flour and fold in a little at a time.
5. Pour into a 10-inch (25-cm) cake tin which has been buttered and floured.
6. Bake in a 350°F (180°C) oven for about 30 minutes. Cool cake and cut in half. Spread frosting between layers and on top and sides of torte.

Apricot Frosting
(Ghiacciata di Albicocca)

2 cups confectioners' sugar
7 tablespoons apricot jam
2 tablespoons brandy
2 tablespoons cream

Combine all ingredients and mix well.

Italian Cookies
(Biscotti)

5 cups flour	1 cup (250 g) butter or margarine
1½ cups confectioners' sugar	3 eggs
2 tablespoons baking powder	1 tablespoon vanilla

1. Sift together flour, sugar and baking powder into a large bowl.
2. Add butter or margarine and mix thoroughly.
3. Add eggs and vanilla and mix to a firm dough. Knead on a floured board for five minutes.
4. Shape into small balls and place on a greased cookie tin.
5. Bake in a 450°F (230°C) oven for about ten minutes.

Makes 5 dozen.

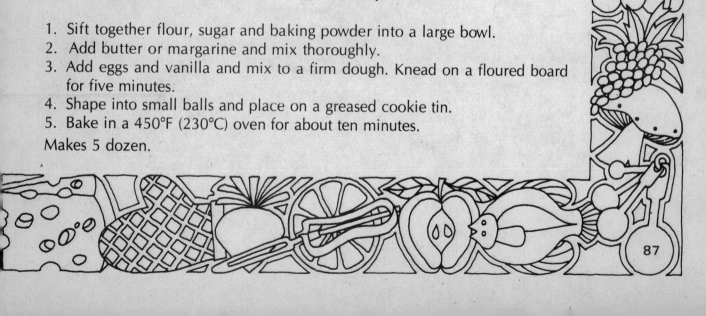

Chocolate Pudding (Budino al Cioccolato)

½ lb (250 g) unsweetened chocolate, grated
4 cups (1 liter) milk
¼ cup flour
1 cup sugar
1 cup (250 ml) cream, whipped

1. Combine the chocolate and milk in a saucepan. Cook over a very low heat until the chocolate is dissolved.
2. Mix together the sugar and flour in the top of a double boiler.
3. Slowly pour on the chocolate milk, stirring constantly.
4. Place over simmering water and continue stirring until mixture thickens. Cool.
5. Pour into an oiled ring mold and chill until set.
6. Unmold and serve with whipped cream.

Serves 6.

Yellow Cake
(Torta Giallo)

6 egg yolks
1 cup sugar
grated rind of one orange
grated rind of ½ lemon
¼ cup (62.5 g) butter or
   margarine, melted

1 cup sifted cake flour
confectioners' sugar

1. In the top of a double boiler mix together egg yolks, sugar and grated rinds. Place over hot water and beat mixture constantly until it is warm. Remove from heat.
2. Add butter or margarine and sifted flour and beat thoroughly.
3. Pour into two 9-inch (23-cm) cake pans which have been well-buttered and floured.
4. Bake in a 350°F (180°C) oven for about ½ hour. When cooked, remove immediately from the pans. Sprinkle with confectioners' sugar.

Sponge Cake
(Pan di Spagna)

6 eggs, separated
½ cup sugar
1½ tablespoons lemon juice
grated rind of one lemon

2 tablespoons sherry
1 cup cake flour
½ teaspoon salt

1. Beat egg yolks until thick and light yellow colored.
2. Add sugar, lemon juice, lemon rind and sherry and beat until light and fluffy.
3. Sift flour and fold into egg mixture gently but thoroughly.
4. Beat egg whites until foamy, add salt and beat until stiff. Fold into batter.
5. Pour into lined and buttered cake pans.
6. Bake in a 350°F (180°C) oven for about 50 minutes.

Zabaglione

6 egg yolks
6 tablespoons sugar
1 cup (250 ml) Marsala

1. Beat the eggs in the top of a double boiler.
2. Beat in the sugar and the Marsala and place over simmering water.
3. Beat constantly until mixture thickens.
4. Pour into individual dishes and serve immediately.

Serves 6.

Gelato

2 cups (500 ml) water
2 cups sugar
pinch of salt

1 cup (250 ml) lemon juice
grated rind of one lemon
2 egg whites

1. Mix together water, sugar and salt in a saucepan. Bring to a boil and cook over a medium heat for five minutes.
2. Strain lemon juice and add with the grated rind to the sugar mixture. Cool.
3. Beat egg whites until stiff and fold into the cooled lemon mixture.
4. Pour into freezing tray, cover with plastic wrap and freeze until firm.

Serves 6.

Fruit Cake
(Panforte)

½ cup cake flour
3 tablespoons cocoa
1½ teaspoons cinnamon
½ teaspoon mixed spice
½ teaspoon nutmeg

½ cup sugar
½ cup honey
¼ lb (125 g) almonds
¼ lb (125 g) mixed dried fruit
½ cup preserved citron

1. Sift flour with the cocoa and spices.
2. Mix sugar and honey in a saucepan and boil for three minutes, stirring constantly. Remove from heat.
3. Quickly stir in flour mixture and remaining ingredients.
4. Spread into a lined 9-inch (23-cm) square pan.
5. Bake in a 300°F (150°C) oven for about 30 minutes.

Christmas Eve Cake
(Torte Vigilia di Natale)

1 cup (250 ml) water
1 cup (175 g) raisins
¼ cup (30 g) chopped walnuts
¼ cup (40 g) chopped almonds
1 cup sugar
½ cup (125 g) butter or
margarine

1 egg
2 teaspoons vanilla
1 teaspoon baking powder
½ cup sifted flour

1. Mix together water, raisins, walnuts and almonds in a saucepan and bring to a boil. Reduce heat and simmer for five minutes. Cool.
2. Cream together butter or margarine and sugar until light and fluffy. Add egg and beat well. Add vanilla.
3. Sift together the baking powder and flour and add to creamed mixture. Mix well.
4. Add fruit mixture and blend thoroughly.
5. Pour into a well-buttered and floured 8-inch (20-cm) square pan.
6. Bake in a 350°F (180°C) oven for about 30 minutes.

Baked Apples
(Cottura al Forno)

6 cooking apples
6 teaspoons brown sugar
1 teaspoon grated lemon rind
¼ cup (40 g) chopped raisins
¼ cup (35 g) chopped dates
1 cup (250 ml) Marsala

1. Core apples and place in a buttered baking dish.
2. Mix together brown sugar, lemon rind, raisins, and dates.
3. Fill the apples with this mixture. Pour Marsala into apples and over the top.
4. Bake in a 375°F (190°C) oven for about 40 minutes, or until apples are soft. Baste frequently with wine.
5. Serve warm with sauce poured over the top.

Fruit in Marsala
(Frutta al Marsala)

1 cup sugar
½ cup (125 ml) water
juice of one lemon

½ cup (125 ml) Marsala
8 small peaches, peeled
2 oranges, peeled and sliced

1. Dissolve the sugar in the water and lemon juice in a saucepan. Bring to a boil and cook until thick. Cool.
2. Add Marsala and chill.
3. Blanch the peaches by plunging quickly into boiling water. Remove from boiling water, drain and peel.
4. Stir peaches and oranges into the syrup and chill thoroughly before serving.

Serves 4.

Rice with Oranges
(Budino di Riso con Arance)

Rice:
¾ cup (155 g) uncooked rice
2 cups (500 ml) milk
½ cup sugar
1 teaspoon vanilla
½ cup (125 ml) cream
3 tablespoons Kirsch

Oranges:
2 oranges
1 cup (250 ml) water
⅔ cup sugar
4 tablespoons Kirsch

1. Combine the rice, milk, sugar and vanilla in a saucepan and simmer until tender. Cool.
2. Whip the cream until thick. Add the Kirsch. Stir into cooled rice mixture.
3. Peel the oranges (reserve the peel from one orange) and slice thinly.
4. Mix together water, sugar and orange peel in a saucepan and boil until it is a syrup. Remove from heat and cool. Strain.
5. Stir in Kirsch and orange slices. Chill.
6. Pour rice pudding into a serving bowl and when ready to serve, arrange orange slices on top.

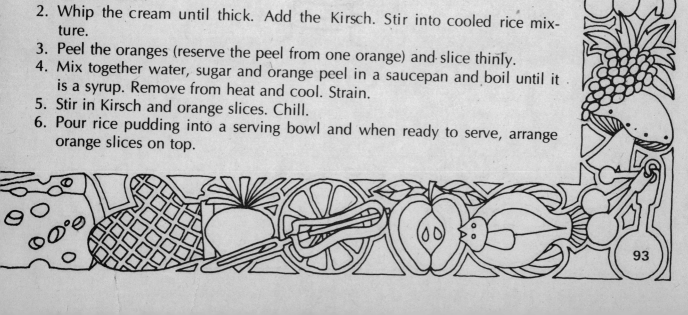

Nut Cookies
(Dolce di Noci)

1 cup (250 g) butter or margarine	2 teaspoons vanilla
1½ cups confectioners' sugar	4 cups sifted flour
3 eggs	1 lb (500 g) chopped nuts

1. Cream together butter or margarine and sugar until light and fluffy.
2. Add eggs, one at a time, beating well after each addition.
3. Add vanilla and mix well.
4. Stir in sifted flour and nuts.
5. Shape into small rolls the size of a finger and place on a greased cookie tin.
6. Bake in a 350°F (180°C) oven for about 10-15 minutes.

Makes about 4 dozen.

Index